Managing Creativity and Innovation

The Harvard Business Essentials Series

The Harvard Business Essentials series is designed to provide comprehensive advice, personal coaching, background information, and guidance on the most relevant topics in business. Drawing on rich content from Harvard Business School Publishing and other sources, these concise guides are carefully crafted to provide a highly practical resource for readers with all levels of experience. To assure quality and accuracy, each volume is closely reviewed by a specialized content adviser from a world-class business school. Whether you are a new manager interested in expanding your skills or an experienced executive looking for a personal resource, these solution-oriented books offer reliable answers at your fingertips.

Other books in the series:

Finance for Managers
Hiring and Keeping the Best People
Managing Change and Transition
Negotiation
Business Communication

HARVARD
BUSINESS
ESSENTIALS

Managing
Creativity and
Innovation

Harvard Business School Press | *Boston, Massachusetts*

Library of Congress Cataloging-in-Publication Data
Harvard business essentials : managing creativity and innovation.
p. cm.—(The Harvard business essentials series)
ISBN 1-59139-112-1 (alk. paper)
1. Technological innovations—Management.
2. New products—Management.
3. Creative ability. I. Series.
HD45.H3427 2003
658.5'14—dc21
2003005543

The paper used in this publication meets the requirements of the American National Standard for Permanence of Paper for Publications and Documents in Libraries and Archives Z39.48-1992.

Contents

Introduction

Back in the 1920s, a young 3M researcher named Dick Drew visited an auto body repair shop in St. Paul, Minnesota. 3M made and sold sandpaper, and Drew had gone to this shop to test a new batch. As he entered, workers were standing around an automobile cursing a blue streak. The problem was a botched paint job. To deal with the two-tone cars popular at that time, auto body workers had to apply one color at a time, masking the other surfaces with butcher paper, which was held in place with a heavy adhesive tape. In this case—and apparently many others—peeling off the tape also peeled away part of the new paint job, creating a botched job and many hours of rework.

Drew might have said, "That's too bad" and gone about his business—testing the new batch of sandpaper. Instead he observed his customer's problem and perceived the need for a tape with a less powerful adhesive—one that would keep the butcher paper in place yet peel off without taking the paint with it. As a maker of sandpaper, his company had some adhesive know-how, but could it make one that would work on a paper tape in the way he envisioned? Would the company be interested?

Drew returned to the 3M laboratory and began a long search for materials and a manufacturing process that would solve the peeling paint problem he had observed—and others like it. Progress, however, was slow. At one point, then-president William McKnight told Drew to get back to work on his primary mission: improving sandpaper. But Drew persisted through an underground campaign that diverted time and funding from his work on abrasives. McKnight eventually realized that his researcher was not following orders, but never called him on the carpet. This was fortunate for 3M, as Drew was closing in on an innovation that would put it on the map.

After two years of experimenting with different papers and adhesive formulas, Drew's persistent quest resulted in a successful new product: masking tape. That product has generated revenues for 3M for over seven decades. More important, it spawned 3M's adhesive tape business, which currently produces more than 700 specialized products for medical, electrical, home, and industrial applications. And Dick Drew became quite a hero at 3M—an icon and model for succeeding generations of 3M managers, technicians, and researchers.

The example set by Drew also made a lasting impression on his boss, William McKnight, who went on to develop management practices designed to encourage innovative behavior among employees and to ensure that Drew's breakthrough with masking tape—and later with cellophane tape—would not be a singular event, but something that Drew and other employees would repeat again and again. McKnight's goal was to create a climate in which innovation would be both natural and sustained. He succeeded in most respects. By 2001 the company had grown into a global enterprise with over $16 billion in annual revenues and leading positions in a diversified set of markets. And innovation on many fronts had fueled that growth over the decades.

You and the people in your organization should have the same goal as William McKnight. You should create a climate and structure within which innovation is encouraged, facilitated, and rewarded. This book offers ideas on how you can succeed in that task. It will not make you an expert, but it will give you the information you need to be more effective in stimulating innovation and creativity in your organization and capturing their benefits.

The Role of Innovation in Enterprise

Innovation valued by the marketplace has long been recognized as a creator and sustainer of enterprise. Every time Intel's engineers produce a new generation of computer chips that its customers value, its fortunes are renewed. Immediate customers such as Dell, IBM, Toshiba, and other personal computer makers quickly snap up the new chip and, by doing so, offer faster and more powerful machines to their customers.

But innovation can also destroy. More than a half-century ago, economist Joseph Schumpeter described the economic, sociological, and organizational impacts of innovation and its "winds of creative destruction." Those winds sweep away both old ways of doing things and the enterprises and institutions that cling to them. During the nineteenth century, innovations in mass production doomed local shoemakers, dressmakers, and many other artisans. We see that pattern repeated today as superstores such as Home Depot, Borders, and Staples decimate the ranks of small local hardware stores, independent booksellers, and office supply retailers, respectively. Likewise, innovations in electronics, pharmaceuticals, and other fields—including services—continually undermine established products and services. Enterprises that fail to keep pace with these innovations are quickly swept from the field.

The Innovation Process

Many managers, technical professionals, and scholars see innovation as a process like the one mapped in figure I-1. That process begins with two creative acts: idea generation and opportunity recognition. In the first, a person develops an insight about something new. Idea generation sometimes takes the form of a technical insight with no apparent commercial application. In most cases, however, a problem or an opportunity inspires the insight. For example, the ruined paint job observed by Dick Drew stimulated the thinking that eventually led to masking tape. More recently, conventional thinking about the performance limits of silicon-based semiconductors inspired IBM researcher Bernard Meyerson to experiment with a silicon germanium alloy. In so doing, he managed to break through the theoretic computing speed barrier and produce a far superior product.

FIGURE I-1

The Innovation Process

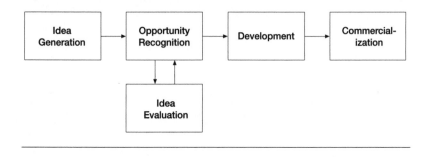

Opportunity recognition occurs when someone says, "This material we've invented might be of value to customers," or "If we could solve this problem, we could create value for our customers and our shareholders," or "This might produce a huge cost advantage."

Once an opportunity is recognized, the idea must be incubated to the point at which it can be evaluated by decision makers, who need answers to several questions:

- Will the idea work?

- Does the company have the technical know-how to make it work?

- Does the idea represent value for customers?

- Does the idea fit well with company strategy?

- Does it make sense from a cost perspective?

Ideas that produce affirmative answers to these questions and that obtain organizational support are moved into some form of idea development and down a long and bumpy road toward commercialization. Some make it to the end of that road, though most do not. Commercialization is the final test for these ideas. Here, customers make the final evaluation.

Creativity plays a critical role in the innovation process. Creativity sparks the initial idea. It also helps to improve the idea as it moves forward.

What's Ahead

Harvard Business Essentials: Managing Creativity and Innovation examines the early stages of the innovation process and the creativity that fuels it. Its goal is to make you and your organization more creative and more effective on the all-important innovation front. It is not a book on new product development—a related subject—though one chapter describes how innovative ideas can be leveraged through product platforms.

Chapter 1 sets the stage with a working definition of innovation and discussion of its different types: incremental and radical; innovations in products, processes, and services. The next chapter describes the S-curve, a concept used by technologists and scholars to describe the life cycle of technologies. Typically, that curve characterizes an early period in which performance improvements or cost reductions, or both, are frequent and dramatic. These occur less frequently as time passes and the technology matures. The S-curve contains a number of lessons for technologists and managers. These are spelled out with examples.

Chapter 3 examines the first stage of the innovative process: idea generation. Where do good ideas come from? The chapter identifies four sources: new knowledge, customers, lead users, and "empathetic design." Readers will also learn the role of skunkworks, and how management can encourage idea generation. The information in this chapter naturally leads to the subject of chapter 4, opportunity recognition. That chapter will help you with the second stage of the innovation process: recognizing when ideas have business value. A method is provided, as is a "rough cut" approach to quantifying an idea's value to the company.

Once an idea is recognized as a business opportunity, it must be moved toward the marketplace, the subject of chapter 5. Here you will learn about tools used by leading companies to determine which ideas they will kill and which they will place their bets on and support through development and commercialization. Among these tools are the stage–gate system of development and review, portfolio analysis, market analysis, and financial assessment using discounted cash flow analysis. Finally, the text shows how innovations that prove their value can be extended more broadly in the marketplace by incorporating them into product or service platforms.

Up to this point, little has been said about the creativity from which innovations emerge, or about things that managers can do to encourage creativity among individuals and teams. We turn to these topics in chapter 6, which examines popular myths about creativity, keys to unlocking it, and a section on the characteristics of creative groups. Chapter 7 pursues the creativity issue further by offering six things that management can do to enrich the organizational environment, making it more conducive to creative thought and action. It also considers the physical workplace, indicating how the co-location of project teams, better communications, and the redesign of workplace features can spark creativity.

Smart and creative people are capable of producing innovative ideas, but their talents are wasted in the absence of strong and thoughtful leadership. Chapter 8 indicates what leaders must do to encourage and make the most of innovation in their organizations. As this chapter makes clear, they must assume responsibility for the culture in which people work. It's their job to develop a culture that welcomes creativity and innovation. No one else can do it. They must also establish the strategic direction for the organization and the boundaries within which new ideas should be developed. Leaders must also participate in the innovation process, particularly in its early stages, when they can have the greatest influence on the design and direction of innovative projects. This requires senior managers to be visible and to act as recognizers and patrons of promising ideas.

We've supplemented these chapters with two appendices. Chapter 5 introduces discounted cash flow (DCF) analysis, a financial tool based on time-value-of-money concepts. This is a tool that many companies use to evaluate incremental innovation projects. Appendix A provides more information on DCF and how it can be directly cal-culated. It also introduces several related concepts, all of which are valuable in assessing the economic merits of innovations or new products: net present value, internal rate of return, hurdle rate, and sensitivity analysis. If you're not already familiar with these concepts, this is a place where you can get an introduction.

Appendix B contains three forms that you may find useful when planning and encouraging innovation. All are adapted from Harvard ManageMentor®, an online help source for subscribers. For interac-tive versions of these worksheets, please visit http://www.elearning. hbsp.org/businesstools. The tools consist of the following:

1. **Workplace Assessment Checklist.** How friendly is your work-place to creativity and innovation? This handy checklist will help you make an assessment.

2. **Assessing the Psychological Environment.** You can use this checklist to assess how your current reward structure, group norms and attitudes, and management style support creativity.

3. **Planning for Innovation.** Innovation is an outcome of the cre-ative process and involves identifying and implementing a new idea. Use this tool to help plan how an idea will be rolled out and to identify the critical factors needed for it to be accepted.

You'll find two other supplements at the end of the book. The first is a glossary of terms. Every discipline has its own special vocab-ulary, and creativity and innovation are no exceptions. When you see a word italicized in the text, that's your cue that it's defined in the glossary. The second supplement, For Further Reading, identifies books and articles that can tell you more about topics covered in this book. If you want to learn more, these publications can help you.

The content of this book is greatly informed by a number of books, articles, and online publications of Harvard Business School Publish-ing, in particular, articles in *Harvard Business Review,* and the "Manag-ing Creativity" module of Harvard ManageMentor, an online service.

1

Types of Innovation

Several Types on Many Fronts

Key Topics Covered in This Chapter

- *Incremental and radical innovation*

- *The factors that favor incremental innovation*

- *Innovation in processes and services*

T HE MEANING OF "innovation" is revealed by its Latin root, *nova,* or new. It is generally understood as the introduction of a new thing or method. MIT professor Ed Roberts once defined innovation as invention plus exploitation. Here's a more elaborate definition: *Innovation* is the embodiment, combination, or synthesis of knowledge in original, relevant, valued new products, processes, or services.

However you define it, innovation takes a number of forms. This chapter acquaints you with each and helps you see how they can help or challenge your business.

Incremental and Radical Innovation

Innovation scholars generally point to two different types of innovation: incremental and radical. *Incremental innovation* is generally understood to exploit existing forms or technologies. It either improves upon something that already exists or reconfigures an existing form or technology to serve some other purpose. In this sense it is innovation at the margins. For example, Intel's Pentium IV computer chip represents an incremental innovation over its immediate predecessor, the Pentium III, since both are based on the same fundamental technology. The Pentium IV simply incorporated design improvements that enhanced chip performance. The same can be said for the navigation devices based on global positioning satellite (GPS) technology that are found in many luxury automobiles; these are less innovations than the application of existing GPS technology to a new use.

A *radical innovation,* in contrast, is something new to the world, and a departure from existing technology or methods. The terms *breakthrough innovation* and *discontinuous innovation* are often used as synonyms for radical innovation. More recently, Harvard professor Clayton Christensen has used the term *disruptive technology* to describe a technical innovation that has the potential to upset the organization's or the industry's existing business model. In almost all cases, these innovations are radical. Disruptive technologies displace the established technology and precipitate the decline of companies whose business models are based on them. In many instances, disruptive technologies create new markets. Those markets are initially small, but sometimes grow large.

The transistor technology developed at Bell Labs represented a radical innovation that disrupted the electronics industry's dominant players, which, at the time, were deeply committed to vacuum tube technology. The same could be said for jet propulsion during the 1940s, when piston-powered engines dominated aviation. Likewise, the silicon germanium (SiGe) chip technology developed by IBM in the late 1990s represented a radical innovation. SiGe chips had four times the switching power of conventional silicon chips and could operate with much less power, making them ideal for applications in new generations of cell phones, laptop computers, handheld digital devices, and other small, portable devices.[1] Likewise, the digital imaging technology used in today's consumer and professional cameras represents a radical departure from the chemically coated film technology upon which George Eastman built the Eastman Kodak Corporation over a century ago.

A team of researchers at Rensselaer Polytechnic Institute defined a radical innovation more specifically as an innovation with one or more of the following characteristics:[2]

- An entirely new set of performance features

- Improvements in known performance features of five times or greater

- A 30 percent or greater reduction in cost

One could add to this list one of the characteristics cited by Lee A. Sage and the PACE Awards program for innovation in the auto industry:

• Changes the basis of competition[3]

Within industries, incremental and radical innovations go hand in hand. The course of innovation is generally characterized by long periods of incremental innovation punctuated by infrequent radical innovations. For example, in electronics, we observe the introduction of vacuum tubes, which were displaced by transistors, which were in turn largely displaced by the semiconductor. Each of these major transitions represented a great leap forward but was followed by a period of steady incremental improvements that gradually enhanced performance, lowered cost, and reduced size. Figure 1-1 represents a theoretical timeline in which radical and incremental improvements take place. Note in this simplified illustration how progress is made through small incremental improvements until radical innovations appear. Progress then takes an abrupt leap forward. Incremental innovation then resumes.

FIGURE 1-1

An Industry Timeline of Radical and Incremental Improvement

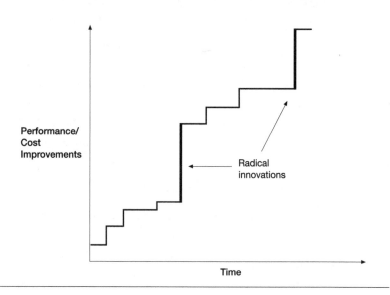

Radical ideas are always in the works somewhere—in R&D labs or in the minds of scientists or entrepreneurs. They usually take a long time to germinate and develop. Their appearance in the marketplace (though most never make it to that point) is both infrequent and generally unpredictable. Incremental innovation follows in radical innovation's train, usually after what Michael Tushman and Charles O'Reilly have called a "period of technological ferment":

> During this period of ferment, competing technological variants, each with different operating principles, vie for market acceptance. The competition occurs between the existing and the new technology (e.g., between tuning forks, quartz, and escarpment oscillation in the watch industry) as well as among variants of that new technology.[4]

These periods of ferment are confusing and uncertain to both producers and customers. In the absence of technical standards, producers don't know which of several new courses to follow (e.g.,VHS or Beta-Max formats; the Mac operating system or DOS/Windows). Customers are paralyzed over the choice of staying with the old technology, switching to the new, or waiting for the dust to settle. We observe that happening today as consumer ask themselves, "Should I buy a digital camera now, or wait for technical improvement and image storage standards to take hold?" or "Should I buy a new large-screen TV or wait for improved digital TV?" Once the dust does settle, and a dominant technical format emerges, incremental innovation and improvement resumes.

At this point you may find it useful to think about the course of innovation in your own industry. Looking back over the past ten years or so, can you identify innovations that really changed the basis of competition? Which innovations would you describe as radical, and which were clearly incremental? Now look to the present:

- Are you aware of any radical innovations in the works that will affect your industry?

- If and when those innovations enter the marketplace, how will they affect competition?

- How might these innovations affect your own company's sales and profitability?

Factors That Favor Incremental Innovation

Radical innovations have the potential to change the basis of competition in favor of the innovator. For example, IBM's introduction of the electric typewriter signaled the end for all manual typewriter makers in the office market and gave it a commanding share of the office market for decades. Henry Ford's innovations in automobile design and assembly likewise changed the nature of the emerging auto industry and gave his company a hold on the market that no one would break for over fifteen years.

Despite the advantage of radical innovation, it presents companies with several serious challenges. Projects dedicated to radical innovation are risky, expensive, and usually take many years to produce tangible results—if they produce results at all. Research by Richard Leifer and colleagues on eleven radical innovation R&D projects indicated that at least ten years were required to show tangible results.[5] To be successful, companies must have the patience and the budgets to support these long timelines. The problems associated with risk, expense, and long timelines encourage most established companies to pursue incremental innovation. It's safer, cheaper, and more likely to produce results within a reasonable time.

Incremental innovation handled systematically provides business units with the steady streams of new, improved, and varied products they need to grow and stay competitive. Incremental innovators must, however, observe two cautions:

1. **Avoid the "more bells and whistles" syndrome**. Pressed by marketers to churn out new versions every few years, many product developers simply add features even though few customers want them. This practice irritates most users and creates a future market for true innovators who produce something simpler and more elegant. For example, every new version of today's office application software suites is bigger, more expensive, and more difficult to master than its predecessor—but offers few tangible benefits for most customers. Customers complain, but have no alternatives. Someday, an innovator may provide an alternative that consumes less memory, is competent, less expensive, and easier

to master. (We may be observing something analogous in the growing success of Linux, which for many is becoming an alternative to the larger, more complex Windows operating system.)

2. **Don't put all of your chips on incremental innovation.** Yes, investments in incremental innovation are less risky and produce results more quickly. But they will not create a bridge between the current and the future generations of technology. Nor will they alter the competitive game in your favor. Only radical innovation can do that. So find a balance in your pursuit of incremental and radical innovations. When a game-changing innovation eventually appears, you want it to be one of your own inventions.

Innovations in Processes

People are used to thinking of innovation in terms of physical, manufactured goods such as computer chips, flat screen displays, fuel cells, night vision equipment, and so forth. In reality, process and service innovations are just as important in the competitive life of companies and industries. Consider the example of the "mini-mill," first developed by Nucor Corporation under the leadership of Ken Iverson. At the time, steelmaking was a mature business involving huge capital assets and supply chains that stretched back to distant ore mining and coal producing operations. Sheet steel was produced by a process that poured mattress-sized slabs of white-hot metal, then gradually reduced slab thickness through a long and expensive series of rolling mills and reheating operations.

Nucor's innovation was to license a then-unproven German technology for continuous casting of thin metal slabs. Sheet steel produced through this technology needed very little milling or reheating. The company also opted to use scrap steel melted in an electric furnace as its raw material, eliminating the need for costly blast furnaces. Continuous casting had been an objective of steelmakers for almost a century, but until Nucor's breakthrough, no one had been able to make it work on a commercial level. Nucor's process innovation not only worked, it ultimately cut the cost of steelmaking by more than 20 percent and changed the competitive framework of the industry.

Process innovations have also played competition-changing roles in glassmaking, petroleum refining, chemical manufacturing, brewing, and many other industries. In many cases, process innovation aims to lower unit production costs, as in the steel example just described. It often does so by reducing the number of disconnected process steps (see "Lowering Costs Through Step Reductions").

Lowering Costs Through Step Reductions

In his study of the plate glass–making industry, James Utterback provides an illuminating example of how costs can be reduced when innovators find ways to reduce the number of disconnected process steps.

Plate glass was traditionally produced through a series of separate steps: mixing and melting the ingredients in a furnace; casting a glass ingot in a mold; annealing the ingot in a special oven; and, finally, grinding and polishing the ingot using successively finer abrasives. This process was slow, laborious, and intensely expensive. Over the years, innovators in the glass industry found ways to integrate or mechanize various steps, thus increasing throughput time and reducing unit cost.

The ultimate glassmaking innovation was, as described by Utterback, the "float glass" process introduced by United Kingdom–based Pilkington Glass in the 1960s. That process integrated all the tasks of glassmaking into a single automated step. Raw materials poured into a furnace at one end became a continuous ribbon of molten glass, which, after passing through an annealing oven, emerged as a finished product at the other end. The costly grinding and polishing step was entirely eliminated.

Pilkington's innovation so reduced the cost of production that the float glass process quickly displaced all other approaches, giving the company a major competitive advantage.

SOURCE: James M. Utterback, *Mastering the Dynamics of Innovation* (Boston: Harvard Business School Press, 1994), 106–116.

The Product–Process Connection

It's one thing to create an innovative new product, but it's another thing to create a process capable of manufacturing it at a price the target market will accept. Thus, innovation in both realms is connected; some innovative products must await process innovation before they can achieve market traction.

The product-process connection is nicely illustrated in the case of the now-ubiquitous disposable baby diaper. Versions of this product first appeared in North America in the mid-1950s, during the postwar baby boom, when the market for this product was huge. Nevertheless, these products failed to gain more than a 1 percent market share. The reason, as research eventually determined, was twofold: poor performance and price.

When Cincinnati-based Procter & Gamble entered the field, its R&D people very quickly solved the performance problem using more suitable materials and a new design. That was the easy part. Developing a cost-effective process for manufacturing its new diaper proved to be a far greater challenge, and one that held back market rollout for longer than anticipated. One engineer described P&G's quest for an effective diaper-making process as the most complex operation the company had ever faced.[6] The company encountered the same problem years later when it attempted to develop its ersatz potato chip, Pringles. Here again, the product idea was relatively simple and straightforward; developing the production process was the real challenge.

Service Innovations

Service is another area in which innovation plays a key role. Great things happen when people rethink how best to serve customers. Service innovation sometimes produces winning business models. Here are just a few notable examples:

- **Dell Computer Corporation.** Dell's PCs are very good, but they share the same technologies as machines offered by competitors. What originally set this company apart and gave it a competitive edge was its innovative strategy of skipping the middleman and selling customer-configured PCs directly to buyers. Later innovations in supply-chain management made this strategy fast and effective—and made Dell the world's most successful PC maker.

- **Southwest Airlines.** Herb Kelleher and his associates built this popular and profitable business through an innovative value proposition to customers: low fares, frequent service, and fun. Kelleher initially developed his service concept to compete with automobile and bus transportation in the Texas regional market. It succeeded there and was expanded elsewhere around the United States, making Southwest America's most profitable airline.

- **Zipcar.** This young company has created an alternative to automobile ownership for urban dwellers in several U.S. cities. Its mission is to offer members affordable 24-hour access to private vehicles for short-term round-trips. When a member needs a car for that occasional trip to the suburbs or for weekly grocery hauling, she reserves one on the Web, goes to one of the many locations where Zipcars are parked, unlocks the vehicle with her Zipcard, and drives away. Payment is based on time and mileage.

Thus, physical product companies are not the only innovators. Many service-driven companies have long and admirable histories of innovation. But not every service innovator succeeds. Consider the fate of Streamline, a Boston-based company whose business model aimed to provide cost-effective, high-quality home delivery of groceries, dry cleaning, prepared meals, shoe repair, and many other household items. The concept was great, and its inventors supported it with Internet connectivity, a fleet of vans, and a state-of-the-art distribution center. But for all its appeal, Streamline went bankrupt. So did WebVan, an even more ambitious enterprise using a similar business model. In both cases, the product idea was appealing, but the process for delivering value to customers either failed or proved too costly.

So if you've developed an innovative service, don't assume that your job is finished. Give as much or more attention to the process that supports it. Think carefully about every step that goes into the production and delivery of your service. Then try to think of how each could be improved (incrementally), combined, or replaced entirely (radically) by something better, faster, and less costly.

Summing Up

This chapter began with a working definition of innovation as the embodiment, combination, or synthesis of knowledge in original, relevant, valued new products, processes, or services. It then described the two major categories within which innovations fall: incremental and radical.

Incremental innovation exploits existing forms or technologies. It either improves something that already exists, making it "new and improved," or reconfigures an existing form or technology to serve some other purpose. The GPS position locators found in many luxury automobiles are examples of an existing technology adapted to a different purpose.

A radical innovation is something new to the world. Many radical innovations have the potential to displace established technologies, as the transistor did when first introduced into the world of vacuum tubes, or to create entirely new markets, or both.

When compared with radical innovation, incremental innovation takes less time and involves less risk, which explains why managers favor it. Incremental innovation alone, however, cannot ensure a company's future competitiveness.

Radical and incremental innovations often operate hand in hand. Thus, the introduction of a successful radical innovation is often followed by a period of incremental innovations, which improve its performance or extend its application.

The chapter underscored the importance of process innovations, which are often overlooked. Process innovations generally aim to achieve substantial reductions in unit costs of production or service delivery. In many cases this is accomplished by integrating or eliminating separate process steps.

Product and process innovations also go hand in hand. As demonstrated by the case of the disposable baby diaper, a breakthrough product often fails to gain market acceptance until a low-cost process for manufacturing it at acceptable quality levels is created.

Finally, service innovation, as exemplified by Dell Computer, Southwest Airlines, and Zipcar, was examined. As with product innovators, service innovators were urged to think carefully about the processes that support production and delivery of their services.

2

The S–Curve

A Concept and Its Lessons

Key Topics Covered in This Chapter

- *The S-curve concept*

- *Lessons from the S-curve for innovators*

WHETHER you pursue innovation through incremental or radical means, you'll eventually run up against practical constraints that either impede further progress or make it prohibitively expensive. This chapter uses the S-curve to describe these situations.

The S–Curve Explained

The course of successful technological innovation is often described through an S-shaped curve like the two shown in figure 2-1. An *S-curve* is plotted on a two-dimensional plane and describes how the performance or cost characteristics of a technology change with time and continued investments. Here the horizontal axis reflects the unfolding history of technical innovations (time and investment), while the vertical axis indicates some particular dimension of product performance or cost competitiveness.

The S-curve of the established technology is on the left in figure 2-1, and the curve of its newer rival is on the right. Notice how the performance of the established technology has improved over time, at first rapidly and then at a modest pace. By the time the rival technology first enters the picture (T1), the established technology is much improved and approaching its maturity.

With maturity, the pace of improvement slows. Years of experimentation and incremental improvements have exhausted most of

FIGURE 2-1

The S-Curve: An Established Technology and a New Rival

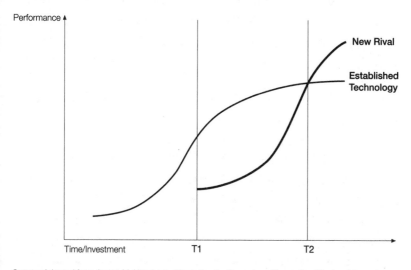

Source: Adapted from James M. Utterback, *Mastering the Dynamics of Innovation* (Boston: Harvard Business School Press, 1994), 158.

the opportunities to improve cost and performance. In other words, the proverbial low-hanging fruit have been picked. Every incremental improvement is more and more costly.

Typically, the newly emerged rival technology is crude when compared with the established technology, with many issues yet unsolved—that's what we see at T1 in the figure. These weaknesses cause established companies to write it off as "not a real threat." Most customers likewise ignore the new technology because it lacks the performance or cost characteristics they require—at least at the moment. The first-generation roll film cameras developed by George Eastman late in the nineteenth century fit this description. The images produced by Eastman's roll film couldn't hold a candle to the superb images produced by chemically coated glass plates, the technical standard of that era. Therefore, the professionals and serious amateurs who constituted the market overwhelmingly rejected

Eastman's product. The same can be observed with respect to many of the innovative high-tech products introduced over the years. If you used the first-generation word processing program for Apple's personal computer, you probably said, "I think that I'll hang onto my old typewriter." And with good reason: That early word processor had only uppercase letters, and the printers available at the time were expensive and produced low-quality output.

History tells us that the first typewriters were even less satisfactory. Samuel Clemens (also known as Mark Twain) was one of the first typewriter owners and complained often about its shortcomings. As he wrote to his friend W. D. Howells of Cambridge, Massachusetts, "I DONT KNOW WHETHER I AM GOING TO MAKE THIS TYPE-WRITING MACHINE GO OR NTO [sic]."

Many of the problems first associated with a new technology, however, are gradually solved over time. Manufacturing process improvements and large-scale production cause costs to fall. Thus, the performance/cost characteristics of the new technology improve with time and investment. That movement is typically slow in the beginning, but picks up speed. At a certain point (T2), the new technology matches its older rival in performance or cost features or both. But unlike the established technology, the new one has plenty of opportunities for continued improvement. If all goes well, it will improve to the point that its older rival will be displaced from the main marketplace.

Barring some unforeseen technical breakthrough, this appears to be the plight of chemical-based photography today as it faces the challenge of digital imaging. The low- and medium-hanging opportunities for film improvement have been exploited. Those that remain will be costly and difficult to exploit. Meanwhile, digital imaging can look forward to many years of technical improvements. It's already happening. Digital cameras are now available for professional and consumer applications. Prices are dropping, and performance gets better every year. It's very conceivable that digital photography will eventually dominate, with film photography surviving only in a number of specialized niches.

Initially, the new technology cannot challenge its established rival directly. Instead, it serves niche markets and *lead users* who for one reason or another value it highly. For example, the hybrid-powered cars first introduced by Honda and Toyota are revolutionary in concept—major departures from the century-old internal combustion engine technology that dominates the existing auto fleet. When first introduced in 2000, these hybrid-powered vehicles lacked some of the performance characteristics (acceleration and top speed) cherished by most drivers. But for the minority of motorists who really cared about fuel economy and the health of the ecosystem, traditional performance characteristics didn't matter. These customers were willing to take a risk on this new technology, and even pay a premium for it. As a result, hybrid cars have found a niche. As the technology improves and as more drivers familiarize themselves with these new automobiles, it's likely that their sales will expand and take a larger share of the broader market. If this happens it will be fairly typical of how successful innovations eventually push out established rivals.

Successful innovations can also gain markets by following paths of diffusion:

- From military to civilian applications (e.g., GPS technology)

- From professional/scientific to consumer uses (e.g., digital imaging)

- From early-adopter "techies" to lagging adopters who are nontechnical and use the innovation in nontechnical ways (e.g., personal computers)

Three Lessons

The scenario described by the two curves in figure 2-1 points to important lessons for business managers. Here we use the terminology of Richard Foster in describing companies associated with the established technology as "defenders" and advocates of the emerging technology as "attackers."[1]

Lesson 1: Defenders Face Difficult Choices

Companies that live off an established technology face difficult choices:

1. Abandon the business they already own, with all its cash flow and certainty, in favor of the rival technology

2. Hold onto what they have and work hard to make it better or useful to more customers

3. Hold onto the existing business *and* begin investing in the new technology as a hedge against the future

Of these options, the first is the most difficult and is almost always impractical. How could any company afford to walk away from its current investments in skills and physical assets? The new technology usually requires new internal competencies and new manufacturing facilities. The customer base may even be different. Dropping everything to jump onto the new S-curve would be financial suicide in most cases. Also, commitment to the new S-curve is required exactly when doing so is most perilous—when the technology is still relatively crude.

Option 2—stick to the current technology—is the easiest choice for decision makers. In the short run it produces no severe disruption, and it is quite possible that improvements to the current technology may extend its competitive life for a number of years. The gas lighting industry managed to do this even as it developed new markets for its product (see "The Gas Industry Fights Back"). But in the long run, sticking with an aging technology almost guarantees that the company will experience declining fortunes.

The third option—hold onto the existing business *and* invest in the new technology—is often the most promising course of action. The company can continue to operate the existing business and serve current customers as the new business develops. This is what Kodak is currently attempting as digital photography rises to challenge its existing film and photo processing businesses. It is the choice RCA, Sylvania, and others attempted decades earlier when their vacuum tube businesses were threatened by the appearance of solid-state transistors. The choice seems logical, but it has practical problems:

The Gas Industry Fights Back

As described by James Utterback in his engaging book *Mastering the Dynamics of Innovation*, the many gas companies that produced and distributed gas for illuminating America's towns and cities enjoyed a comfortable monopoly until the 1880s, when incandescent electric lamps appeared. Recognizing the threat, the gas companies fought back with incremental improvements to gas production and distribution. They also launched a public relations campaign that emphasized the dangers of electricity, and used their political influence to impede electric distribution. These tactics, however, did little to hold back adoption of electric lighting.

The gas industry got a big break when Austrian inventor Carl von Welsback created a mantle that produced a fivefold improvement in gas lighting efficiency and a one-third reduction in operating costs. "This single improvement," writes Utterback, "threatened to sink the nascent electric light industry and explains why it took Edison twelve years to turn a profit in his fast-expanding electric lighting business."

Welsback's improvement gave gas lighting new life—but only briefly. Subsequent improvements were few and insignificant. Meanwhile, electric lighting was making regular and substantial improvements in cost and performance. Gas was doomed as a form of lighting. But the industry survived and prospered by finding new markets in residential and commercial heating and process heat for industry.

SOURCE: James M. Utterback, *Mastering the Dynamics of Innovation* (Boston: Harvard Business School Press, 1994), 64–66.

- **The company may not have the competencies to develop the new technology.** The film photography business, for example, is based on deep knowledge of chemicals, papers, and process technologies; digital photography demands knowledge of advanced electronics.

- **The culture of the organization may not welcome the new technology.** IBM ruled the world of mainframe computing, and mainframe people ruled IBM. So when the decision was made in the 1980s to develop a PC business to serve the growing desktop computing market, that business was never treated seriously.

- **Existing customers may pressure the company to stay in the old business.** Many, if not most, customers have a strong bias toward the established technology and will stick with it until the new one is demonstrably superior and less costly. Until that time they urge companies to continue supplying them with parts and upgrades—in effect, to stay in their old businesses. Some call this phenomenon the "tyranny of served markets."

In many cases the best solution to these practical problems is for the established enterprise to develop the new technology within a separate subsidiary or operating unit. Clayton Christensen put it this way in an interview about his book, *The Innovator's Dilemma:*

> *With few exceptions, the only instance in which mainstream firms have successfully addressed a disruptive technology were those in which the firm's managers set up an autonomous organization charged with building a new and independent business around the disruptive technology. Such organizations, free of the power and influence of the mainstream company's customers, can align themselves with a different set of customers—those who* want *the product of the disruptive technology.*[2]

Lacking an autonomous organization, the business formed around the disruptive technology faces the danger of being killed, undermined, or sold by internal rivals and naysayers. This is easy to understand when one considers that the concerns of the established business and of the new business are poles apart. Worse, the new business will be evaluated by managers of the mainstream business—and by their standards, which are profits and efficiency. The day-to-day concerns of these managers are diametrically opposed to those required by the innovative business, as shown in table 2-1. The new business typically fails to meet any of the standards of the mainstream business. So when the mainstream managers who run the place meet to discuss the

TABLE 2-1

Comparison of Management Concerns for New and Mainstream Businesses

Concerns of the New Business	Concerns of the Mainstream Business
Innovation	Control
Risk taking	Predictability
Market acceptance	Operating efficiency
	Profit margins

future of the new business, it's not unusual for them to say, "This is draining investment funds from our profitable businesses. Let's pull the plug." Or, "It has potential, but not for us. Let's find a buyer."

IBM attempted to avoid this problem when it first decided to produce a desktop computer, which entered the market in 1981. It set up a *skunkworks* operation in Boca Raton, Florida, far from company headquarters, and gave its managers autonomy in designing and developing their product. GM did the same when it entered the small car market in a serious way. It established Saturn as a separate operation, located it far from Detroit, and gave its managers a fairly blank slate on which to design their vehicle, production system, and labor-management relationship.

The danger, of course, is that these autonomous operations will be absorbed back into the parent organization as soon as they show signs of success—before they reach a point of self-sustaining development.

Lesson 2: Leaders in One Generation of Technology Are Seldom Leaders in the Next

Given the problems with each of the choices described earlier, it is not surprising that leaders of one generation of technology are seldom leaders of the next. The electronics business provides a fitting example, as described by Tushman and O'Reilly:

In the mid-1950s, vacuum tubes represented roughly a $700 million market. Leading firms . . . included such great technology companies as RCA, Sylvania, Raytheon, and Westinghouse. Yet from 1955 to 1982, there was almost a complete turnover in industry leadership, a remarkable shakeout brought on by the advent of the transistor.[3]

The same phenomenon has been observed in many other industries. Here are a few examples:

- When mini-computers came along, upstart Digital Equipment became the leader, not IBM, the then-dominant computer company.

- General Motors and Ford dominated the U.S. auto market. When small, efficient vehicles became popular in the 1970s, leadership swung to foreign producers.

- Swiss watchmakers dominated their industry until the advent of quartz technology (a Swiss invention). Most Swiss companies disappeared or were forced to retreat into luxury timepiece niches as Asian watches swept the market.

These examples may be disheartening if your company currently leads its industry. Although long-term decline is likely, it is not inevitable. Defenders, according to Richard Foster, can enlist various strategies to defeat upstart technical challengers:

- **Leapfrog the attacker's technology.** During the early stage of the S-curve, a new technology and its markets are undeveloped. If the attacker is a small company with limited resources, full development may be slow in coming. That leaves the large defender with greater resources an opportunity to jump onto the S-curve and get ahead of its competitor.

- **Acquire the attacker.** If the attacker's new technology appears poised to eat up your business, consider buying the attacker. If you follow this course, however, be sure to give the acquired company the autonomy it needs to succeed. Alternatively, consider licensing the attacker's technology.

Lesson 3: Attackers Enjoy Important Advantages

New technologies and innovative business models are often introduced through small, entrepreneurial firms. These firms, in fact, form around new technologies or business models. Hewlett-Packard, DEC, Intel, Apple, Microsoft, Amgen, Southwest Airlines, Dell, Sun, and eBay all began in this way.

Though entrepreneurial firms are generally weak in terms of brand recognition, manufacturing, and financing in their early stages, they often enjoy substantial advantages. Here are the most important:

- **An undivided focus.** Managers of upstart companies spend little time on internal operations and people issues: There are very few of either. Instead, they devote most of their attention to development of the new technology or business model.

- **An ability to attract talent.** Capable technical and managerial talent are often attracted to new ideas with promising futures, especially when stock options are a significant portion of compensation.

- **They are not captives of powerful customers.** Many established companies fail to make the leap to the new technology because powerful customers persuade them to continue doing what they are doing. This is what happened to Goodyear Tire and Firestone when radial tire technology appeared. Not wanting to change their suspension designs, the Big Three U.S. automakers urged their suppliers to stick with bias ply tires. Michelin, which had no supplier relationship with the Big Three, pressed forward, establishing leadership in the field. Attackers are seldom the pawns of customers.

- **Little bureaucracy.** Almost by definition, small entrepreneurial companies are unencumbered by the bureaucracy that burdens their larger rivals. That makes them fast and flexible.

- **No need to protect investments in unrelated skills or assets.** Established companies can find many reasons to not adopt new technologies or business models: "We can't sell it through our existing distribution network." "It would cannibalize our current sales." "We just invested $50 million in facilities to manufacture our current product." "Our salespeople wouldn't understand it; they'd have to be retrained." Attackers seldom have these concerns.

Where Do You Stand on the S-Curve?

Return for just a moment to figure 2-1. Where does your company stand on the S-curve? Is it at the point where every incremental improvement to its products, services, or technology is more and more costly to produce and less and less important to customers? If this describes your company, you're at or near an end-game situation.

Now think about the new, rival S-curve. Is your company being challenged by a new technology? If it is, do you still enjoy performance or cost advantages? Is that advantage likely to last as the rival technology is perfected? If you answered "no" to that last question, your company must change or face decline. It has several options:

1. Get on board the rival technology—perhaps by acquiring the innovator company.

2. Leapfrog the rival technology with something better.

3. Look for a breakthrough that will give your technology a new lease on life.

4. Stick with your current technology, but expand it into different markets.

Limits to These Lessons

The S-curve is a useful thinking tool for managers. It describes generalized development paths for new and established products and technologies. But use it with this important caution: Nothing about these paths is preordained; not every innovation overcomes its established rival. Indeed, we could fill a book with descriptions of innovative technologies that appeared promising but failed to make a real dent in the market. Gallium arsenide, for example, hasn't made a dent in silicon-based chip business, as many had forecasted. Optical storage hasn't bested its entrenched magnetic rival as many predicted. And the list goes on. So look before you leap from one S-curve to another.

Summing Up

This chapter explained the concept of the S-curve and its implications for managers and innovators. Here are the key points:

- An *S-curve* describes how the performance or cost characteristics of a technology change with time and continued investments. In the generalized model, a newly introduced technology is crude and not particularly competitive with established rivals, except in specialized niche markets.

- Performance or cost characteristics or both enjoy a period of rapid and steady improvement as technical issues are solved. Eventually, the innovation's performance or costs may equal—and perhaps exceed—those of the established rival.

- Eventually, the new technology enters a period of maturity in which improvements are small, infrequent, and increasingly costly. At this point it become vulnerable to attack by still newer technologies.

The S-curve concept was shown to have a number of lessons:

1. Defenders face difficult choices with respect to how they should react to the appearance of a new technology.

2. Leaders in one generation of technology are seldom leaders in the next.

3. Attackers enjoy important advantages over established rivals: an undivided focus, an ability to attract talent, freedom from the

"tyranny of service markets," little bureaucracy, and no need to protect investments in unrelated skills or assets.

To grasp the lessons of the S-curve, managers should do the following:

- Stand back and contemplate where their companies and their key technologies are on the S-curve.

- Do the same for rival technologies, particularly those with promising futures.

- Determine which strategic option is most promising.

3

Idea Generation

Opening the Genie's Bottle

Key Topics Covered in This Chapter

- *New knowledge as a source of innovation*

- *Tapping the ideas of customers*

- *Learning from lead users*

- *Empathetic design*

- *Generating ideas through invention factories and skunkworks*

- *Open market innovation*

- *The role of mental preparation*

- *How management can encourage idea generation*

I NNOVATIVE IDEAS have many sources. Some originate in a flash of inspiration. Others are accidental. But as Peter Drucker told readers of *Harvard Business Review* almost two decades ago, most result from a conscious, purposeful search for opportunities to solve problems or please customers.[1] His observation supports Thomas Edison's famous judgment that invention is ninety-nine percent perspiration and one percent inspiration.

This chapter examines six sources of innovative ideas: new knowledge, customers, lead users, empathetic design, invention factories and skunkworks, and the open market of ideas. It goes on to discuss the important role of mental preparation, and what management can do to generate more good ideas.

New Knowledge

Many, if not most, radical innovations are the product of new knowledge. Consider the computer. It is the product of new knowledge in the areas of binary mathematics, symbolic logic, programming concepts, and various technical breakthroughs, including the audion electronic switch. Likewise, IBM's innovative silicon germanium chip resulted from laboratory findings that contradicted accepted wisdom on certain properties of that alloy. That chip has now found important new uses in electronic gadgets where processing speed and low power consumption are critically important.

Although innovations based on new knowledge are often powerful, there is generally a lengthy time span between development of new knowledge and its transformation into commercially viable products. The computer took over fifty years to surface in the market. Satellite communications took even longer. Considering all the elements that are required to launch and maintain earth satellites—knowledge of calculus, physics, electronics, and aeronautical science—we can say that the timeline of satellite communications stretches back several hundred years to Newton and Kepler.

Despite the time lags involved with new-knowledge-based innovations, the rewards are often enormous. Consider Corning's development of fiber optics technology, which that company now dominates. Corning scientists began learning about the light-transmitting properties of glass—"light pipes" as they called them—in 1966, but it wasn't until 1970 that a team of its scientists produced a material capable of transmitting electronic impulses at the levels required by standards of the day. It took many more years before the new materials found a place in the market.

Tapping the Ideas of Customers

Customers are an evergreen source of innovative ideas if salespeople, service people, and R&D workers listen to what they say and probe for more. Customers, for example, are often the best source of information on the weaknesses of current products: "It's a great device, and I'd use it more often if it would fit in my briefcase." (Idea: Make the device smaller.)

Customers can also be the best source for identifying unsolved problems: "Our pizza restaurant chain has never been able to generate much luncheon business. It takes too long to prepare and bake a regular pizza." (Idea 1: Develop an oven capable of cutting the cooking time in half; idea 2: Develop a half-prepared pizza product.)

Most companies appreciate the importance of customers as a source of new ideas, and they address that source regularly with market research. You should also. When quizzing customers, however, be less concerned with product or service specifications and more concerned with the outcomes that customers desire. This is the advice of consultant Tony Ulwick, founder of Strategyn. Using the example of music storage media, the outcomes would be "access to a large number of songs, play without distortion over time, resist damage during normal use, and require minimal storage space. These are outcomes—not solutions."[2] The next step, according to Ulwick, is to prioritize the list of desired outcomes according to their importance to customers, with each outcome being quantified. For example, research might indicate that "play without distortion" is the most important value, and "resist damage" is the least important.

Beware the Tyranny of Served Markets

Observe one caution in listening to customers: They are capable of diverting you from your pursuit of innovation.

Good businesspeople take the virtue of listening to customers and pleasing them as an article of faith. But sticking too close to current customers can stifle innovation and lock your company into technologies that have no future. This happens when (1) customers fail to understand technical possibilities, and (2) when they are afraid that innovations will render their own systems obsolete. Consider these related examples:

- Market researchers ask a customer focus group to describe the kind of automobile they would like to purchase five years in the future. With limited knowledge of alternative technical possibilities, and with current autos as the reference point, the focus group describes a vehicle very similar to those currently in the showrooms.

- A customer has recently purchased a $10 million hardware and software system from your company. When queried about new ideas, this customer does not encourage you to do anything that might undermine the value of her investment—such as a new-generation computer software system. Instead, you'll be encouraged to incrementally improve the current system.

Some companies compound the "tyranny of served markets" described in the second example by creating review systems that kill ideas and products that their current customers do not want. They focus all their resources on serving today's profitable customers and markets. This almost guarantees that they will produce nothing but slightly improved versions of their current products and services and will surely miss the next big wave of change that alters the competitive environment.

Learning from Lead Users

Lead users are another valuable source of innovative ideas. *Lead users* are companies and individuals—customers and noncustomers—whose needs are far ahead of market trends. They may be pioneering radiologists searching for better methods to produce or interpret scanned images. They may be military pilots, professional athletes, or engineers who have discovered ways of modifying off-the-shelf equipment for substantially higher effectiveness in the field. In all cases, their needs motivate them to produce innovations that suit their unique requirements—often before manufacturers think of them.

Lead users are seldom interested in commercializing their innovations. Instead, they innovate for their own purposes because existing products fail to meet their needs. Their innovations can often be adapted, however, to the needs of larger markets, which will be recognized many months or years in the future.

MIT professor Eric von Hippel was the first to study lead users as a source for innovative ideas. In several of the fields he studied—notably scientific instruments, semiconductors, and computers—more than half of all innovations were made by users, not by product manufacturers. Thus, approaching these lead users and studying their unique applications and product modifications can be an effective substitute for internal idea generation (see "A Four-Phase Process"). As an example, von Hippel suggests that an automotive brake manufacturer might seek out particular users whose requirements for effective braking exceed those of normal users. These might be auto racing teams, producers of military aircraft, or manufacturers of heavy trucks.

A Four-Phase Process

An article coauthored by Eric von Hippel, Stefan Thomke, and Mary Sonnack described a four-phase process used by some 3M units to glean innovative ideas from lead users. This process may also work for you.

1. **Lay the foundation.** Identify the targeted markets and the type and level of innovations desired by the organization's key stakeholders. These stakeholders must be on board early.

2. **Determine the trends.** Talk to experts in the field about what they see as the important trends. These experts are people who have a broad view of emerging technologies and leading-edge application in the area being studied.

3. **Identify and learn from the lead users.** Use networking to identify users at the leading edge of the target market and related markets. Develop relationships with these lead users and gather information from them that points to promising ideas that could contribute to breakthrough products. Use this learning to shape preliminary product ideas and assess their business potential.

4. **Develop the breakthroughs.** The goal of this phase is to move preliminary concepts toward completion. Host two- to three-day workshops with several lead users, a small group of in-house marketing and technical people, and the lead user investigative team. Work in small groups and then as a whole to design final concepts.

SOURCE: Adapted from Eric von Hippel, Stefan Thomke, and Mary Sonnack, "Creating Breakthroughs at 3M," *Harvard Business Review,* September–October 1999, 47–57.

Empathetic Design

One of the problems that innovators face in determining market needs is that target customers cannot always recognize or articulate their future needs. Because most are unaware of technical possibilities, they tend to identify their needs in terms of current products and services with which they are already familiar. They express their needs in terms of incremental improvements to these products and services: a thinner laptop, an automobile with better fuel economy, a TV screen with better resolution, faster service.

To generate innovations that go beyond improvements to the familiar, you must identify needs and solve problems that customers may not yet recognize. Empathetic design is a technique for doing this. *Empathetic design* is an idea-generating technique whereby innovators observe how people use existing products and services in their own environments. Harley-Davidson uses this technique when it sends engineers, marketing personnel, and even social anthropologists to HOG (Harley Owners Group) events. These employees observe how Harley owners use and customize their bikes, the problems they encounter, and so forth. Those observations become the raw materials for innovative ideas. Following this same strategy, a Japanese consumer electronics company sent a young engineer to live with an American family for six months to observe how they cooked their meals, communicated with friends, and entertained themselves. Those observations were used to create new consumer products.

Some companies take this approach very seriously. IDEO, a leading product design company, bases its design process on an anthropologic approach. Procter & Gamble, a prolific new-product producer, does also. It trains all new R&D personnel in what it calls "Product Research," the P&G approach to observing how customers use products in day-to-day life. The goal is to put people who have knowledge of technical possibilities and design in direct contact with the world experienced by potential customers.

As described by Dorothy Leonard and Jeffrey Rayport, empathetic design is a five-step process:[3]

1. **Observe.** As described previously, company representatives observe people using products in their homes and workplaces. The key questions in this step are: Who should be observed, and who should do the observing?

2. **Capture data.** Observers should capture data on what people are doing, why they are doing it, and the problems they encounter. Because the data are frequently visual and nonquantifiable, use photographs, videos, and drawings to capture the data.

3. **Reflect and analyze.** In this step, observers return from the field and share their experiences with colleagues. Reflection and analysis may result in returning people to the field for more observations.

4. **Brainstorm.** This step is used to transform observations into graphic representations of possible solutions.

5. **Develop solution prototypes.** Prototypes clarify new concepts, allow others to interact with them, and can be used to stimulate the reactions of potential customers. Are potential customers attracted by the prototypes? What alterations do they suggest?

As you can well imagine, empathetic design is critically important when you're developing consumer products for nondomestic markets, where preferences for product size, colors, and applications may be quite different from those preferred by the home market.

Invention Factories and Skunkworks

Many large manufacturers generate and develop innovative ideas through formal research and development units—innovation factories, if you will. Some enterprises support R&D at two levels: the corporate level and the business unit level. Generally, corporate-level R&D works on radical innovations and enabling technologies that various operating units can use. Bell Labs provides an example. Over its seventy-five-plus years of operation, Bell Labs has produced a stream

The Wizard's Invention Factory

Today we are accustomed to the idea of corporate and university research centers—well-equipped and funded laboratories where teams of scientists and technicians conduct research and development on tomorrow's breakthrough technologies. Nothing like this existed, however, until the late 1800s, when Thomas Edison systematized the business of innovation.

Edison set up his first R&D center in Menlo Park, New Jersey, in 1876 with the goal of developing technologies and inventions with commercial potential. As a way of pursuing innovation, this was itself an innovation. Using his earnings from previous inventions (such as the stock ticker) and investors' capital, he set up shop in a facility that included a long two-story clapboard building, a smaller brick mechanical shop, some small sheds, and a farmhouse. He stocked these buildings with technical books, machining equipment, laboratory instruments, electrical testing devices, and chemicals, and staffed them with more than forty capable mechanics and technicians.

Within five years, Edison had outgrown Menlo Park and moved to a larger facility in West Orange, New Jersey. But during that short period he and his associates had patented four hundred inventions and churned out a number of important commercial successes (as well as some spectacular failures), including the carbon transmitter for the Bell telephone; the phonograph; the tasimeter, a supersensitive heat-measuring device; and the incandescent electric lamp. Thomas Edison became known as the Wizard of Menlo Park. More important, Menlo Park created a model for modern industrial research.

SOURCE: Adapted with permission from James M. Utterback, *Mastering the Dynamics of Innovation* (Boston: Harvard Business School Press, 1994), 59–60.

of scientific and technical breakthroughs, including the transistor, the laser, and the UNIX computer operating system. Currently part of Lucent Technologies, Bell Labs has a twofold mission: basic research in scientific fields related to communications, and the development of leading-edge products and services. This mission is typical for corporate-level R&D.

R&D at the business unit level, in contrast, focuses on incremental innovations that will benefit the unit directly and in the short term. Business unit managers with profit-and-loss responsibilities are either unable or unwilling to shoulder the financial burden of long-term radical innovation projects. They look to corporate R&D for those.

In their study of eleven radical innovation projects, Leifer and coworkers found that business units were happy to accept an innovation handoff from the corporate R&D lab, but only *after* most of the expensive and time-consuming work had been done.[4] Idea generation at this level aims to improve the performance of the mainstream business—and that usually means a focus on incremental innovation.

A formal R&D program is not the only structure for creating innovative ideas. Some companies have generated ideas by temporarily bringing together talented people with different perspectives for the sole purpose of solving a particular problem. In some cases, these individuals are sited in remote settings to keep team members focused on their mission, to minimize interference from the rest of the organizations, or to maintain secrecy. The term *skunkworks* is often applied to these focused project teams. Lee Sage found one such situation at Johnson Controls, Inc. (JCI), a major supplier of vehicle interiors to the auto industry. Besides its corporate mission, JCI had a dual goal of using more recycled materials and producing zero landfill wastes. To further that goal, it wanted to create a new material for its products and chose to do so through a skunkworks project. As told by Sage: "[T]he company identified 30 engineers it viewed as competent and creative in the materials area, set them up in an unused company building in Holland, Michigan, and asked them to come up with a new and suitable car interior material."[5]

JCI's skunkworks eventually produced CorteX, an energy-absorbing material made from recycled plastic soft drink bottles and carpeting. CorteX found its way into vehicle overhead systems, door panels, and other auto interior features developed by the company. This idea–generation experience was so successful that JCI adopted it again—this time for a one-year project to create innovations in vehicle seats.

Tips on Where to Look for Innovative Ideas

Are you having trouble finding innovative ideas for your business? Every one of the ideas sources described in this chapter can help you. Other places to look include the following:

- **Wherever a new technology and customer needs intersect.** GPS technology was developed for military navigation. This technology and the need of auto drivers to know their map locations relative to their destinations created a new option on luxury automobiles.

- **Demographic change.** An aging population has prompted some home builders to examine how they design kitchens, bathrooms, and closets from the perspective of aging residents—people who may have trouble reaching high shelves, negotiating steps, and getting in and out of showers.

- **Market change.** The big Wall Street firms laughed when Charles Schwab created his no-frills discount brokerage service. Schwab correctly recognized that more and more successful baby boomers were developing nest eggs and looking for places to put them. His do-it-yourself brokerage service appealed to many of these boomers.

- **Unexpected occurrences.** George Eastman was crestfallen when photographers dismissed his first great invention—celluloid roll film. It wasn't up to their standards. That rejection inspired Eastman's second great invention: photography for the masses. Using his roll film and inexpensive box cameras, he turned Americans—and then the world—into picture takers.

Open Market Innovation

Not everything must be "invented here." Innovative ideas can often be acquired (or sold) in the open market.

Bain & Company's Darrell Rigby and Chris Zook coined the term *open market innovation* to describe how companies can reach outside for the ideas they need for new products and services. As explained by Rigby and Zook in a *Harvard Business Review* article, open market innovation employs licensing, joint ventures, and strategic alliances to bring the benefits of free trade to the flow of new ideas.[6] An example can be found in the actions of Pitney Bowes—a major producer of mail metering systems—when confronted with the anthrax scare that first hit the United States in late 2001. The company had no ideas about how to help customers whose mail and employees were at risk. Needing ideas and solutions fast, it looked outside for help. With the collaboration of outside inventors, it quickly developed scanning and imaging technologies capable of spotting contaminated letters and packages.

According to Rigby and Zook, open market innovations have four distinct advantages:

1. Importing new ideas can help you multiply the "building blocks" of innovation.

2. Exporting ideas is a good way to raise cash and keep talent.

3. Exporting ideas gives companies a way to measure an innovation's real value.

4. Exporting and importing ideas helps companies clarify what they do best.

There are, of course, risks associated with collaborating across organizational boundaries. Key among them is the danger of failing to adequately capitalize on ideas that you share with others in the open market. The best safeguard against this danger is a deal structure that protects your interests.

A Lab Accident Leads to a Major New Product

The value of a prepared mind is illustrated by the invention of 3M's fabric protector, Scotchgard, whose development was triggered by a 1953 laboratory accident. As described by the company, one of its researchers was conducting fluorochemical polymer experiments when a lab assistant accidentally spilled some of the solution on her tennis shoes. The researcher tried removing it without success. She tried soap and water, alcohol, and other solvents, but nothing worked. As often happens in cases where the participants have technical training, keen powers of observation, and native curiosity, a light went on in her mind. She reasoned that if the substance was resistant to solvents, it also might protect textiles from stains. Further development of the substance led to a successful new product.

The Role of Mental Preparation

Although it's true that many ideas are generated unintentionally through random observations, routine contacts with customers, and even unintended laboratory results, it's also true—to quote Louis Pasteur—that "chance favors the prepared mind." A prepared mind is more likely to formulate a problem-solving idea or recognize an opportunity (see "A Lab Accident Leads to a Major New Product").

Preparation is often cited as the first step in the creative process that leads to innovation. To prepare themselves for idea generation, would-be innovators should immerse themselves in the problem at hand. As suggested by one expert on managing creativity, they should do the following:[7]

- Search the literature.

- Look at all sides of the problem.

- Talk with people who are familiar with the problem.

- Play with the problem.

- Ignore the accepted wisdom.

How Management Can Encourage Idea Generation

If innovation is a key function of companies, then management has a responsibility to encourage the generation of innovative ideas. Both traditional and nontraditional tools can be used for this task. These tools include rewards, a climate of innovation, hiring innovative people, encouraging the cross-pollination of ideas, and providing support for innovators. Let's consider each in detail.

Rewards

Reward those who generate ideas with pay or promotions or both. It's a clear signal that good ideas are important. Monetary rewards appear to be more effective when they are performance based and when they give employees a personal stake in organizational success. Many innovative companies, 3M being one example, use dual career ladders—technical and managerial—to reward innovative behavior. They realize that not everyone is cut out to be a manager, nor do some people wish to be.

Rewards for innovators, however, should encompass more than pay and promotions. Monetary rewards and promotion prevent feelings of abuse—that is, of being taken advantage of—but they do not drive the free thinking needed for innovation. For many people the rewards that lead to innovation emphasize greater freedom: freedom to explore hunches, to pursue one's curiosity, to travel to technical conferences, to mingle with customers and lead users, and so forth. Access to greater resources is also an effective reward when innovation is the goal.

A Climate of Innovation

Management determines the organizational climate. Innovative organizations have these characteristics:

- Management sends a clear message that the well-being of the company and its employees depends on continuous innovation.

- People aren't afraid to try or suggest new things.

- No one feels a sense of entitlement for just showing up for work.

- There is a visceral discomfort with current success—a nagging sense that it may not last.

- People rise and fall on their merits and contributions.

- Employees are outward looking: They seek ideas and best practices among competitors, through professional contacts, and in other industries.

If the climate of your company lacks these characteristics, change it.

Hire Innovative People

Some people are more innovative than others. Ed Roberts and Alan Fusfeld identified the following as personal characteristics of idea generators:[8]

- Expert in one or two fields

- Enjoy doing innovative work

- Usually individual contributors

- Good problem solvers

- Find new and different ways of seeing things

Many of these characteristics can be identified in the normal hiring process—in résumés, hiring interviews, and reference checks. So be on the lookout for them. Look in particular for these individuals: engineers with broad interests, who can bridge the boundaries between technical disciplines; technical people who like to meet customers and wrestle with their problems; and continual learners.

As a general rule it's wise to avoid hiring hyperspecialists—people who want to learn more and more about less and less. Also, avoid hiring anyone who has no interest in customers or their problems.

Encourage the Cross-Pollination of Ideas

Ideas and knowledge produce little when they are isolated in organizational pockets, but something magical happens when those pockets are opened. Formerly isolated ideas come together to produce real opportunities. You can encourage this cross-pollination of ideas by any of the following means:

- Periodically reassign technical specialists to different work teams.

- Send people to professional conferences and scientific convocations.

- Set up an *intra*company knowledge management system—this makes knowledge and experience captured in one area available to everyone.

- Sponsor events that bring outside experts to your company to give lectures and workshops—what they have to share often catalyzes ideas within the company.

- Arrange periodic customer site visits.

- Arrange field trips to observe best practices in other industries.

- Meet with local inventors and entrepreneurs in your field.

- Seek out consultants with different perspectives.

- Seek out university professors on sabbatical to temporarily join your group or participate in brainstorming sessions.

Support for Innovators

Just as artists have always looked to wealthy patrons so that they can be free to pursue their muses, so innovators need the support of highly placed managers. Without that support, many ideas die on the vine.

Management support need not—and often should not—take the form of formal funding and staff resources, particularly in the early stages. But senior managers can provide the resources that innovators need to "bootleg" unofficial development of their ideas: unused space in which to run experiments, small sums for equipment and part-time help, and time away from regular duties in which to pursue an idea.

Senior managers can also protect worthy ideas from the organizational mechanisms that kill off ideas. What are these mechanisms?

- **A negative view of ideas that don't serve existing customers.** This is the "tyranny of served markets" syndrome. Antidote: Remind people that current customers are just a segment of the customer universe. The new idea may be just the ticket for another segment. Also remember that current customers who don't like the new idea may change their tune once the idea is perfected and competitively priced.

- **The new idea threatens the current business.** "If we did this we'd simply cannibalize our existing sales." Antidote: Remember that if you don't eat up your current business with different (i.e., superior) product, someone else will.

- **The market potential seems too small relative to the size of the existing business.** Big companies miss out on many important innovations because the potential is viewed—often erroneously—as too small. "We're a $2 billion company. Why would we want to mess around with something that might only contribute $5 million to sales?" This is a powerful argument, since companies need to maintain focus. Antidote: Remember that many innovations initially appeal to small niches but expand as the technology improves and customers find new and unanticipated uses for it. (Examples: Initial market research on a new-fangled machine called the "computer" indicated world demand for only ten units; the only imagined customers were national defense and scientific organizations. Likewise, the Internet was initially conceived as a communications link for the academic and scientific communities.)

Many organizations create mental blocks to creativity without even realizing it. Table 3-1 is a tool that can be used by you or your group to think about whether the listed items are stumbling blocks that interfere with your creative efforts or are building blocks to creativity that you want to nourish. Add your own ideas or blocks to the list.

TABLE 3-1

Mental Blocks to Creativity

Stumbling Blocks to Creativity	Building Blocks to Creativity
Resource myopia (nearsightedness)	Resourcefulness
Following the rules . . . too closely, too often	Ability to think outside the rules
Seeing play as only frivolous	Playfulness
Focusing on just the right answer	Focus on exploring possibilities
Being judgmental, critical	Being accepting
Fear of failure	Ability to accept failure and learn from it
Discomfort with taking risks	Intelligent risk taking
Difficulty hearing another perspective or opinion	Active listening, acceptance of differences
Lack of openness to ideas	Receptivity to ideas
Political problems and turf battles	Collaboration, focus on mutual gain
Avoiding ambiguity	Tolerance for ambiguity
Intolerance	Tolerance
Lack of flexibility	Flexibility
Giving up too soon	Persistence
Worrying too much about what people will think	Having an inner focus
Thinking you're not creative	Recognizing creative potential in self

Source: HMM Managing for Creativity and Innovation.

Two Idea-Generating Techniques

Companies use a variety of techniques to generate new ideas. We offer two here: brainstorming and catchball.

Brainstorming

Most readers have had some experience with brainstorming. Effective brainstorming is guided by five key principles:

1. **Focus.** Brainstorming should concentrate on a particular problem and be bounded by real-world constraints.

2. **Suspended judgment.** All judging should be suspended while ideas are being generated. Even the wildest ideas should be encouraged.

3. **Personal safety.** Participants should be assured that unpopular ideas or ideas that threaten the status quo will not provoke recriminations.

4. **Serial discussion.** Limit the discussion to one conversation at a time and keep it focused on the topic.

5. **Build on ideas.** Try to build on the ideas of others wherever possible.

Brainstorming techniques fall into several broad categories: visioning, modifying, and experimenting. Each category uses a slightly different thought process, but there are some common features. Modifying and experimenting techniques, for example, start with existing data and use intuitive insights to draw ideas from those facts. Visioning techniques use the intuitive process first and then follow up with information gathering and data analysis.

VISIONING The visioning approach asks people to imagine, in detail, a long-term, ideal solution and the means of achieving it. The goal is to break free of the ingrained practicality that inhibits innovative thought. Once you've generated several ideas that would constitute that ideal solution, ask what it would take to make those ideas happen. Table 3-2 summarizes visioning techniques.

TABLE 3-2

Visioning Techniques

Wish List

Generating wishes

Ask people to "let themselves go" and imagine an ideal situation where, for example, you would be granted any wish you want by a fairy godmother, by winning the lottery and having unlimited resources, or by whatever else sets the tone. Select a quiet place without interruptions, or play soothing background music.

Exploring the possibilities

Encourage everyone to review their lists: What did they discover about themselves or the situation? Then take it another step: What would it actually take to make this wish come true?

The Ideal Scenario

Ask the group to imagine what the ideal future or solution would look like. This can be done with words or with images. For example, participants could pore through visually rich magazines, select images, and paste them together in a collage. Follow the creation with discussion and exploration.

Time Machine

As another alternative, ask participants to pretend that they can time travel to five to seven years from now. What would the situation look like then? What would have been accomplished? Add whatever questions are relevant to the creative challenge being explored.

Source: HMM Managing for Creativity and Innovation.

MODIFYING Visioning techniques begin by assuming that there are no constraints. Modifying techniques, on the other hand, begin with the status quo—with current technology or conditions—and try to make adaptations. One good way to see how your current product or service could be modified is to look at it as though you were a customer. Consider every feature of the product or service and how it adds to or diminishes value for you.

EXPERIMENTING Experimenting helps you to systematically combine elements in various ways and then test the combinations. One such approach involves creating a matrix. For example, a car wash owner in search of a new market or market extension would begin by listing parameters across the top: method, products washed, equipment, and products sold. Under each parameter, he would list

all the possible variations he can think of. Under the equipment category, the variations might include sprays, conveyors, stalls, dryers,
and brushes; the products washed category might include cars,
houses, clothes, and dogs. The resulting table allows the owner to put
together new business possibilities using alternatives listed under the
columns. Thus, he might decide to start a service for boat owners to
wash their boats using the existing stalls and brushes.

Catchball

Among their other contributions to management methods, the
Japanese have given us *catchball*. Catchball is a cross-functional
method for accomplishing two goals: idea enrichment or improvement, and buy-in among participants.[9] Once you've generated an
idea, you can build and improve on it using this method.

Here's how it works. An initial idea is "tossed" to collaborators
for consideration, as in figure 3-1. The idea might be a new strategic
goal, a new product, or a way to improve some work process. Whoever "catches" the idea assumes responsibility for understanding it,
reflecting on it, and improving it in some way. That person then
tosses the improved idea back to the group, where it is again caught

FIGURE 3-1

Catchball Figure

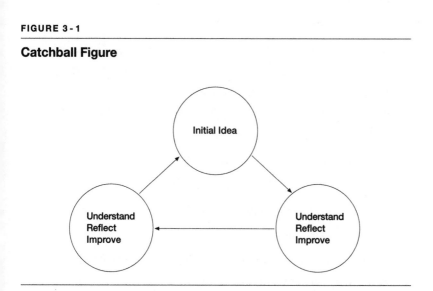

and improved. And around it goes in a cycle of gradual improvement. As people participate, they develop a sense of shared ownership and commitment to the idea that takes form.

Catchball's underlying principle goes back to the Socratic method of dialogue first articulated by Plato. Try using it the next time your organization needs to develop a raw idea and get people committed to it.

Summing Up

Ideas are the nutrients of innovation. You can't get anywhere without them. And in the innovation race, organizations with many good ideas have a real advantage. This chapter has examined key sources of innovative ideas:

- **New knowledge:** Though the trail from new knowledge to marketable products is often long, this is the source of many, if not most, radical innovations.

- **Customers' ideas:** Customers can tell you where current products fall short and can point to unmet needs.

- **Lead users:** People (or companies) whose needs are far ahead of market trends. Look at what they're doing today to meet needs that others will confront tomorrow.

- **Empathetic design:** An idea-generating technique whereby innovators observe how people use existing products and services in their own environments. Try going out and observing how customers and potential customers do things and attempt to solve problems.

- **Invention factories and skunkworks:** R&D labs and special projects with singular missions and their own quarters.

- **Open market innovation:** Free trade of ideas between entities through licensing, joint ventures, and strategic alliances.

The chapter ended with suggestions for how management can encourage idea generation:

- Reward idea generators with pay or promotions or both.

- Create a climate of innovation.

- Hire innovative people.

- Encourage cross-pollination of ideas.

- Provide support.

4

Recognizing Opportunities

Don't Let the Good Ones Slip By

Key Topics Covered in This Chapter

- *A method for recognizing value*

- *Rough-cut business evaluation of opportunities*

- *Tips for enhancing opportunity recognition*

INNOVATIVE IDEAS are exciting. They're fun to uncover and discuss with colleagues. But there's a big difference between an interesting idea and an idea that represents a real business opportunity. Can you tell the difference? Motorola had an idea for using a constellation of satellites to provide cell phone service everywhere on the planet (the Iridium project). It was a neat idea, but, as its development revealed, not much of a business opportunity. In contrast, 3M scientist Art Fry had an idea for using a weak adhesive to make notepaper stick to other things—like his church choir's hymnals. It eventually appeared to represent a business opportunity. After a number of false starts, that opportunity was confirmed, and just about everyone in the white-collar world now has a pad of Post-It Notes in easy reach.

Opportunity recognition is a mental process that answers a question that every innovator must ask: Does this idea represent real value to current or potential customers? Being able to answer this question correctly is probably as important as having an innovative idea or developing a scientific breakthrough. Norman Augustine, former CEO of Lockheed Martin and a great aerospace innovator, put it this way: "The whole idea is to be smart enough to recognize those breakthroughs when they present themselves."[1]

Some innovators have articulated opportunity recognition in memorable ways: "There is an idea that will revolutionize business," Henry Benedict told Philo Remington after seeing a demonstration of the first practical typewriter. "I have struck a big bonanza," wrote Thomas Edison in describing the possibilities tied up with electric lighting.

The opportunities of most innovations are not always obvious. Innovators must ask themselves, "What could we do with this?" This was a question that DuPont's developers of Biomax, a biodegradable polymer material, took several years to answer. Initially, DuPont researchers thought that thin sheets of their interesting new material could be used as liners for disposable baby diapers. But the diaper manufacturers weren't interested. After putting the material on the shelf for a long period, someone thought of using it in the banana groves of Central America, where its ability to protect fruit until it reached harvesting age and then disintegrate into a harmless mulch would be a real benefit. But that didn't prove to be much of a business opportunity either. Since then, many applications have been found for this interesting and versatile material.[2]

Even when an opportunity is recognized, that opportunity may be small relative to the innovation's full potential. This is what happened to radio early in the twentieth century. Inventor Guiseppe Marconi made great strides in wireless telegraphy, as it was called, in the 1890s. The opportunity he recognized for this development was important but limited: ship-to-shore communication. Governments, shippers, and marine insurers were interested, enough so that Marconi could launch a successful business. His innovation is credited with saving thousands of lives at sea: 700 from the 1912 sinking of the *Titanic* alone. But the true commercial potential of radio wave transmission eluded Marconi until 1922, when the first wireless transmission of musical entertainment was made. Suddenly, radio was more than a means of sending Morse code messages between stations; its potential as a broadcast medium for sharing news and entertainment with the masses was finally recognized.

Marconi's narrowly conceived opportunity for radio technology is not unique. The Internet followed a similar trajectory. It was initially conceived as a rapid communications medium for the scientific and academic communities. Its utility for the broader public and for business-to-consumer and business-to-business commerce was only recognized later. In this sense, opportunity recognition is often an unfolding process. The initial window of opportunity is a passageway to others.

A Method for Opportunity Recognition

Recognizing the opportunity associated with an innovation is usually chancy. Data about the innovation's performance in use are either limited or speculative. How customers will respond to a commercial version of the innovation can only be inferred. As a result, many innovators either fail to recognize opportunities or overestimate them. Both errors can be costly.

Although there is no proven formula for opportunity recognition, W. Chan Kim and Renée Mauborgne have described a method called the buyer utility map that indicates the likelihood that customers will be attracted to a new idea or product.[3] Kim and Mauborgne believe in focusing on an innovation's utility—how it will change the lives of customers. The buyer utility map, shown in figure 4-1, helps innovators to think about two things: (1) the levers they can pull in delivering utility to customers, and (2) the various stages in the "buyer experience cycle," which runs from purchase to disposal. Each stage encompasses a wide variety of specific experiences. An innovator can use this map to identify the utility offered by the new product or service at various stages of the buyer experience cycle.

In their article in the *Harvard Business Review*, Kim and Mauborgne offer the example of discount broker Charles Schwab. With 24/7 phone (and later online) service, Schwab created utility in the "convenience-purchase" cell of the matrix. By offering instantaneous trade confirmations over a secure connection, the firm also offered utility in the "risk-purchase" cell.

You can use figure 4-1 to assess the utility of an innovative idea. Ask yourself the following questions:

- Where can we create the greatest utility for our customers? Does our idea fill this space?

- Is that utility higher or lower than the utility created by the products or services offered by our competitors?

- Which of these utilities matters most to customers?

FIGURE 4-1

The Buyer Utility Map

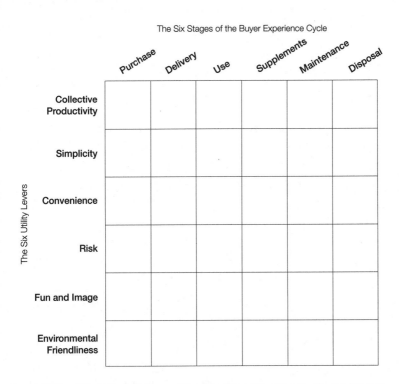

Source: W. Chan Kim and Renée Mauborgne, "Knowing a Winning Idea When You See One," *Harvard Business Review,* September–October 2000, 129–138.

• How could we redesign our product or service idea to offer the greatest utility to customers in the areas that matter most to them?

In answering each question, you can get a good sense of the business potential of an innovative idea.

Rough-Cut Business Evaluation

Let's assume that your innovative idea qualifies as a legitimate opportunity—that is, it has real value for customers. One more task is required before the idea can move forward into development and formal market research: a rough-cut business evaluation. Such an evaluation considers three fundamental questions:

1. Does the innovation have a strategic fit with your company?

2. Do you have the technical competencies to make it work?

3. Do you have the business competencies to make it successful?

Note that a rough-cut evaluation is qualitative. Quantitative idea screening comes later, as the idea becomes more completely formed. At this point, you simply want to determine if some individual or small team should use time and resources to investigate the idea and develop it further.

Strategic Fit

You may have a great idea, but if that idea lacks strategic fit with your company, its development and commercialization could create long-term problems. For example, a new system for making espresso coffee in half the time would not have a strategic fit with broker Charles Schwab, but a new and easy-to-use financial planning software program would. That's obvious; the strategic fit of ideas floating around your company is bound to be much less obvious, so be very thoughtful as you think through the question of strategic fit.

What should you do with a good idea that lacks strategic fit? A good idea, almost by definition, has profit potential for someone. But in ill-equipped hands, that potential may never be realized. Also, pushing into unfamiliar terrain with an innovation is risky. Thus, the choices are threefold: drop the idea, license it to someone who can do something with it, or create a separate or joint-venture organization to develop it. Let's consider the last two.

The motives behind licensing agreements are widely known. Here's a classic example. A small pharmaceutical company develops and gains regulatory approval to produce and sell a new drug, but it has neither manufacturing capabilities nor effective distribution. It determines that its best option is to license manufacturing and distribution to a major pharmaceutical company in return for an upfront payment and a royalty on sales. Thus, the innovator captures value from its invention even though it lacks the capacity to make it successful.

The joint venture operates on the same principle, bringing together complementary resources to capture value. Here, the innovator teams up with an organization that has the missing resources, capabilities, or market access. Working together, the two (or more) organizations have a chance of making a success of the recognized opportunity.

Technical Competencies

Every company has one or more technical competencies. A securities broker-dealer has competencies in trading, market making, and information systems. A mini-mill steel company has technical competencies in metallurgy, manufacturing, and logistics, among others. Does your company have the technical know-how to successfully develop a particular idea? If it does, proceed with the idea. If it does not, could that know-how be acquired?

Business Competencies

Business competencies include marketing, new product development, the ability to serve a particular customer base, the ability to manage widely scattered employees and facilities, and so forth. What are your core business competencies? Are they the same ones your innovative idea will need in order to become successful? If your company lacks any of the required competencies, ask yourself if the idea is big enough to justify the effort and expense of developing those competencies.

**Tips for Enhancing
Opportunity Recognition**

Although opportunity recognition takes place in the minds of
individual employees, management can take steps to facilitate it.
It can

- **Be very clear about company strategy and long-term objectives.** This helps people answer the question "Does my idea
  fit with company strategy?" That question cannot be answered
  if people don't understand the strategy.

- **Expose research scientists and engineers to customers and
  marketing.** This exposure arms the opportunity recognition
  mechanism within these individuals.

- **Give people with ideas a place to take them.** This is one of
  the findings of Leifer and colleagues in their study of radical
  innovation. The "place" is often a business development
  manager who serves as a link between the company's R&D
  efforts and the world of customers and their problems.[4]

Summing Up

This chapter explored the important activity of opportunity recognition, which attempts to answer a fundamental question: Does this
idea represent real value to current or potential customers?

A method for recognizing value was provided, based on Kim and
Mauborgne's buyer utility map, which helps innovators to think
about two things: (1) the levers they can pull in delivering utility to
customers, and (2) the various stages in the buyer experience cycle,
which runs from purchase to disposal.

A rough-cut business evaluation of opportunities is another non-
quantitative screen that separates good ideas from all the rest. It asks
three fundamental questions: Does the innovation have a strategic fit

with the company? Does the company have the technical competencies to make it work? Does the company have the business competencies to make it successful? If you get positive answers to all
three, the idea has potential.

Finally, the chapter suggested several things that management can
do to facilitate opportunity recognition among employees.

5

Moving Innovation
to Market

Will It Fly?

Key Topics Covered in This Chapter

- *The idea funnel*

- *Stage-gate systems—and a caution regarding using them*

- *Financial issues involving innovation*

- *Extending innovation through platforms*

N OT EVERY IDEA with commercial potential makes the challenging journey from the innovator's mind to the marketplace. Even after passing the rough-cut business evaluation described in the previous chapter, subsequent development will find many—if not most—innovations to be either technically unfeasible, too costly to execute, or unacceptable to customers. The high mortality rate of ideas along the development path is a fact of life that innovative companies accept. They recognize the importance of culling weak and inappropriate ideas.

This chapter examines practices used by leading companies to determine which ideas they will kill and which they will place their bets on and support through development and commercialization.

The Idea Funnel

Innovative companies must eliminate unpromising ideas as quickly as possible, before they absorb significant resources. Even those that pass the opportunity recognition tests described in chapter 4 must be screened to identify the strongest and most promising. Learning more about an idea always involves costs—for staff people, for testing, for market research, and so forth. So the quicker a company can kill off the ideas that won't make it to commercialization, the less its costs will be. Quick kills have the virtue of making more resources available for the handful of ideas that have real merit.

Product developers and academics have long used the *idea funnel* as a metaphor for the issues just described. The funnel shown in figure 5-1 has a wide mouth into which many undeveloped and roughly screened ideas are poured. As the funnel narrows, the criteria for staying in the funnel become progressively more rigorous. The process encompasses "tinkering," experimentation, market research, and prototyping. Some ideas survive this winnowing process longer than others, but only a few pass entirely through the funnel toward commercialization.

The funnel concept raises a number of important issues for innovators:

- What should the criteria be for staying in the funnel?

- How long will development and experimentation be allowed to progress before someone pushes the "kill" button?

- How should the kill decision be made?

FIGURE 5-1

The Idea Funnel

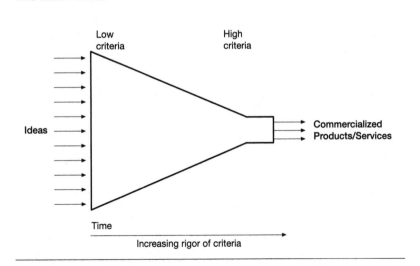

There are no right or wrong answers to any of these questions. But different answers produce different consequences. For example, a company that allows ideas to stay in the funnel for a long time— that is, one that gives ideas every chance to prove themselves—is less likely to mistakenly kill a good idea. However, its costs will be higher than those tallied by a quick-kill company. The slow-to-kill company will also take longer to get its few winners out of the funnel and into commercialization, everything else being equal. This lengthens the entire product or service development process, which generally has negative consequences. Here's the reason: A company has a limited number of people available to evaluate and develop new ideas. The longer it takes these people to evaluate and dispose of an idea, the longer the remaining ideas will sit in the queue. That adds to total cycle time.[1]

The quick-kill company, in contrast, will reduce time and cost in its total development cycle. But its haste in disposing of many innovative ideas may result in the accidental killing of a great idea that people simply do not understand. The probability of making this mistake is greatest with the most innovative ideas, which require more effort to evaluate. A quick-kill approach may also alienate people on whom the company depends to feed the funnel with good ideas. They may stop submitting new ideas if they see their ideas rejected without fair and complete consideration.

Thus, a company must keep one eye on its pool of good ideas and the other on its resources—funds, development personnel, market researchers, and so forth. It must also develop a workable balance in how it rejects some ideas and moves others forward.

Stage–Gate Systems

The idea funnel is a useful means of conceptualizing the way in which many ideas are reduced to the handful with the greatest chance of commercial success. But what goes on inside the funnel? Is there a practical method for deciding which ideas should be killed and which should move forward?

Every company must have a method for sorting good ideas from bad ones. For many companies that method is a *stage-gate system*. The stage-gate system was developed by Robert Cooper in the late 1980s.[2] It is an alternating series of development stages and assessment "gates" that aims for early elimination of weak ideas and faster time-to-market for potential winners. These stages and gates control events from the birth of an idea all the way to commercialization. Figure 5-2 is a generic representation of that system. Here's how it works in practice.

- **Stages:** Phases of the process in which development work is done. For example, a system would have stages for developing the raw idea, technical specifications, a prototype, and so forth. Commercialization is the final stage.

- **Gates:** Checkpoints at which people with decision-making authority determine if the project should be killed, sent back for more development, or advanced to the next development stage. Gates may be used at various points to determine strategic fit, whether the project passes technical and financial hurdles, whether it's ready for testing or launch, and so forth.

A system like this is certainly an improvement over one that is either ad hoc or arbitrary. And for innovators it is certainly superior to

FIGURE 5-2

A Stage-Gate System

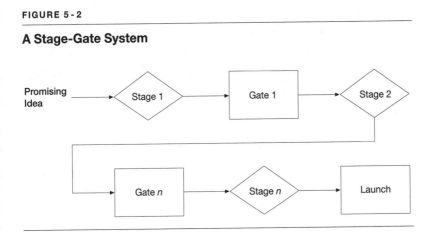

a system in which they must curry favor with powerful executives to keep their projects alive and moving forward. It is also better for companies because, if managed properly, it prevents projects of dubious value from hanging on and soaking up scarce resources that could be applied profitably elsewhere. Many companies have these types of projects, which generally persist because there is no rational system for terminating them. This is where a stage-gate system can help.

The effectiveness of a stage-gate system, however, is no better than the decision-making teams that control each gate. These teams should

- Be experienced with innovation and product development

- Have expertise in the discipline required at their particular gate (e.g., marketing or financial analysis)

- Have the authority to extend or withdraw funding

- Be very clear about company strategy

- Be objective and unencumbered by political pressure

You can probably imagine how the wrong people at various gates can undermine the system. The "wrong" people are those who lack expertise or experience, are there to exert political pressure, or are out of touch with company strategy. Keep these people off your decision teams.

The first gate in any stage-gate system is the screening of what appear to be promising ideas. For the purposes of this book, screening is the most important gate because all others are clearly in the domain of new product development. There is no formula for idea screening, but an article by Robert Cooper suggests that screeners should do the following:[3]

- **Seek a balance between errors of acceptance and rejection.** The chapter discussed this idea earlier. Don't be so conservative that only "sure things" are accepted, and don't be so lax that the company must spread its limited development funds too thinly over many projects.

- **Learn to live with ambiguity and uncertainty.** Reliable data and quantitative measures are almost never available at this early stage.

- **Use decision criteria that reflect the company's objectives.** Also consider the goals of the new product program.

A Caution on Funnels and Stage-Gate Systems

Any process that helps a company sift through its innovative ideas and place its bets on those with the greatest potential must be used with extreme caution because it could, in the long run, put the company on the downward slope toward obsolescence. This caution is underscored by Clay Christensen's warning that many high-performing companies have well-developed systems for killing ideas and products that their customers seemingly don't want. Funnels and stage-gate systems are among them:

> It's part of an entrenched philosophy that focuses resources on the most lucrative markets of the moment. As a result, these companies find it very difficult to invest in disruptive technologies—low margin opportunities that their customers don't want at that time—until their customers realize they want them. And by then it's too late.[4]

This is not to condemn funnels and stage-gate systems per se. These systems may be perfectly serviceable for both incremental innovations that serve existing markets and radical innovations that create new ones. The problem, some companies find, is with the screeners and the go/kill criteria they apply. If a company kills every idea that cannot demonstrate value for existing customers or large existing markets, then few radical ideas will survive. This practically guarantees that the company will not be on the leading edge of the next wave of innovation that washes through its industry. Persistent killing of radical ideas will also signal employees that the company is not interested in doing anything substantially different from what it has done in the past. In other words, "wasting our time and resources with far-out ideas won't help your career at this firm."

One antidote to this problem is to set up a parallel evaluation system to deal with innovations that fall outside of a company's current markets and technologies. That system might have stages and gates, but its gatekeeping teams would be staffed by individuals with broad interests, long time horizons, a solid sense of technical trends, successful track records as innovators or entrepreneurs, and status in the organization.

Financial Issues

Managers and innovators must eventually confront the financial issues bound up in new ideas as those ideas move closer and closer to commercialization:

- How much would it cost to bring the idea to market?

- What price would we ask?

- How many units could we expect to sell at that price?

- What would be our costs of marketing, production, and service?

In its early stages, a radical idea is usually too raw and unformed to examine in terms of these questions. If the idea represents something truly new to the world, any answers would have to be based on sheer guesswork—hence, they would be useless.

The same cannot always be said for incremental innovations. By definition, an incremental innovation is simply a step or two removed from an existing product or service with a measurable market and pricing structure. Furthermore, the cost of developing the new idea, launching it, and filling orders can often be estimated from experience with related products. Thus, innovators and managers can often apply financial tools as they determine which ideas should move forward, be killed, or be sent back for additional development. Two of those tools are explained here: breakeven analysis and discounted cash flow analysis.

Breakeven Analysis

Breakeven analysis tells you how much (or how much more) you need to sell in order to pay for a fixed investment—in other words, at what point you will break even on the cash flow produced by a new product or service. With that information in hand, you can look at market demand and competitors' market shares to determine whether it's realistic to expect to sell that much. Breakeven analysis can also help you think through the impact of price changes and volume relationships.

More specifically, the breakeven calculation helps you determine the volume level at which the total after-tax contribution from a product or an investment covers its total fixed costs. But before you can perform the calculation, you need to understand the components that go into it:

- **Fixed costs:** Costs that stay mostly the same, no matter how many units of a product or service are sold—costs such as insurance, management salaries, and rent or lease payments. For example, the rent on the production facility will be the same whether the company makes ten thousand or twenty thousand units, and so will the insurance.

- **Variable costs:** Those costs that change with the number of units produced and sold; examples include utilities, labor, and raw materials. The more units you make, the more you consume these items.

- **Contribution margin:** The amount of money that every sold unit contributes to paying for fixed costs. It is defined as the net unit revenue minus variable (or direct) costs per unit.

With these concepts defined, we can make the calculation. We are looking for the solution to this straightforward equation:

Breakeven Volume = Fixed Costs / Unit Contribution Margin

And here's how we do it. First, find the unit contribution margin by subtracting the variable costs per unit from the net revenue per unit. Then divide total fixed costs, or the amount of the investment, by the unit contribution margin. The quotient is the breakeven volume, that is, the number of units that must be sold in order for all fixed costs to be covered.

To see breakeven analysis in practice, let's imagine that you have an idea for a new and improved version of your company's vegetable processing machine. After some investigation, you estimate that the company will incur $500,000 in fixed costs in developing the tooling and production lines needed to manufacture this machine. That $500,000 cost will be the same whether the company produces one new and improved vegetable processor or one million. Meanwhile, the marketing people believe that each machine should sell for $75, and the manufacturing department estimates that the variable cost per unit will be $22. Then

$$\$75 \text{ (Price per Unit)} - \$22 \text{ (Variable Cost per Unit)} = \$53 \text{ (Unit Contribution Margin)}$$

Therefore,

$$\$500,000 \text{ (Total Fixed Cost)} / \$53 \text{ (Unit Contribution Margin)} = 9,434 \text{ units}$$

The preceding calculations indicate that the company must sell 9,434 vegetable processors to recover its $500,000 investment.

At this point, the company must decide whether the breakeven volume is achievable: Is it realistic to expect to sell 9,434 additional veggie processors, and if so, how quickly?

COMPLICATION OF BREAKEVEN ANALYSIS Our veggie processor breakeven analysis represents a simple case. It assumes that costs are distinctly fixed or variable, and that costs and unit contributions will not change as a function of volume (i.e., that the sale price of the item under consideration will not change at different levels of output). These assumptions may not hold in the real world. Rent may be fixed to a certain level of production, then increase by 50 percent as you rent a secondary facility to handle expanded output. Labor costs may in reality be a hybrid of fixed and variable costs. And as you push more and more of your product into the market, you may find it necessary to offer price discounts—which reduces contribution per unit. You will need to adjust the breakeven calculation to accommodate these untidy realities.

Discounted Cash Flow

The second financial tool worth considering here is *discounted cash flow (DCF) analysis*. The DCF is based on time-value-of-money concepts that recognize that a dollar received in the future is worth less than a dollar received today. For example, $1.03 received a year from today is worth only $1 if you receive it today. Why? Because a dollar received today could be placed in a risk-free bank account paying 3 percent annual interest. In a year, you'd have $1.03. You understand compound interest; think of DCF as reverse compounding.

This example introduced a number of important terms used in DCF analysis. The $1 is a *present value* (PV), that is, an amount received today. The $1.03 is a *future value* (FV)—the amount to which a present value or series of payments will increase over a specific period at a specific compounding rate. The number of periods (n) in this example is one year. The rate (i)—sometimes called the *discount rate*—is 3 percent. When innovators understand these terms, they are on their way to speaking the same language that senior managers use when they decide to direct or withhold resources from innovative ideas. With a little help from a financial calculator or a preprogrammed electronic spreadsheet, it's possible to calculate present values and future values with ease. (Note: If these concepts are new to you and you'd like to learn more, see Appendix A. It explains time-value concepts and how to calculate them, and provides several examples.)

DCF analysis has many applications in business decision making. Let's consider one that involves a project based on incremental innovation. Rhoda and her team submitted a proposal to Acme Communication's innovation assessment committee to develop a new line of cell phones with built-in GPS capabilities. "Thanks to this new product," said the proposal, "people who talk incessantly on their cell phones while driving will no longer need to keep track of where they are going—a serious problem for 83 percent of people who use cell phones in their vehicles, according to our research. By simply pushing the GPS button on their new 'IdiotFones,' these confused individuals will be able to determine their exact locations at any time of the day or night. Another phone button will automatically dial 911 for emergency service when and if they strike pedestrians while taking those all-important calls."

Acme's senior managers were impressed. But they wondered if the IdiotFone was a good financial bet. Rhoda's team addressed their concern with DCF analysis based on estimates of fixed development costs, manufacturing costs, marketing and selling costs, and anticipated revenues. That analysis, shown in table 5-1, involved a multi-year series of cash flows discounted to their present values using Acme's cost of capital (10 percent) as the discount rate. When discounted to the present and summed, the positive cash flows produced over the first five years exceeded the up-front investment even

TABLE 5-1

Net Present Value of IdiotFone Cash Flow

	Year					
	0	1	2	3	4	5
Cash flows	−400	+50	+70	+100	+150	+200
PV	−400	+45.45	+57.85	+75.13	+102.45	+124.18
NPV (sum of PVs 0–5)	+5.067 or $5,067					

Figures are in thousands. Discount rate = 10 percent. PV, present value; NPV, net present value.

as the project earned its cost of capital, making the IdiotFone proposal something worthy of management attention.

In this simplified example, we see a negative cash flow of $400,000 in year zero—Acme's up-front investment in IdiotFone development and tooling. This is the cash outflow required to get the project off the ground. The company then experiences a positive cash flow of $50,000 *at the end* of the first year, as revenues from phone sales kick in. Larger cash flows follow as IdiotFones become more popular.

To find the *net present value* of Acme's stream of cash flows, one must find the present value of each of the positive cash flows, discounted at 10 percent for the appropriate number of years. By adding together those present values and then subtracting the $400,000 initially invested, we will have the net present value of the investment. As long as that net value is positive, the project earns its cost of capital and more.

Discounted cash flow analysis is a powerful tool, but it must be used with care. The final calculation is only as good as the numbers put into it. In the IdiotFone example, one would ask the following questions:

- Where did the $400,000 investment cost figure come from? How accurate is it? Won't ongoing investment be required to keep the new product line going?

- How accurate are the cash flow estimates for years 1 through 5? Did the project team consult with experienced marketing and manufacturing personnel in developing these numbers?

- What is the level of uncertainty associated with each cash flow estimate? If the estimates are the median values in a range of possible estimates, what are the high and low estimates for each range?

Decision makers would also want to know their alternatives to this investment. Even if they accepted the proposal and its DCF analysis at face value, prudence would dictate that it be considered in the context of competing projects.

Cannibalization Issues

In many cases of innovation—both radical and incremental—development and commercialization of the idea will "cannibalize" some part of the company's existing business. For example, Toyota's hybrid-powered vehicle, the Prius, has attracted a number of buyers with strong interest in the environment or fuel economy. Based on positive auto reviews and feedback from owners, sales of the Prius are likely to grow in the years ahead. But we can assume that some number of these sales will be made to individuals who would have purchased existing Toyota models had the innovative hybrid car not been available. Thus, a certain amount of cannibalization of existing sales will be going on.

Innovators and managers must confront the cannibalization issue as they assess the value of their new technologies and products. In most cases they will conclude that the wisest course is to displace their current products and services; otherwise, competitors will step in to do the job.

Extending Innovation Through Platforms

The concept of product platforms is worth considering because it is a powerful approach to extending innovation into the market. A *product platform,* as described by Marc Meyer and Al Lehnerd, whose work has largely defined this important concept, is "a set of subsystems and interfaces that form a common structure from which a stream of derivative products can be efficiently developed and produced."[5]

The ubiquitous Swatch watch is an example of a successful product family based on a common platform. The Swatch platform is a small set of timepiece subsystems linked together through a few electronic interfaces. This platform is, in effect, the innovation. Almost every Swatch uses the same platform, which is simple, inexpensive to manufacture, and capable of supporting endless external variations. As an innovation, this platform saved its maker, Societé Micromécanique et Horologerè (SMH), from business failure and helped it produce watches for fashion-oriented consumers with different tastes.

Product platforms based on design elegance and manufacturability give companies low-cost opportunities to customize their products for different market segments, as shown in figure 5-3. In this figure we see how the platform of common elements can be joined with some unique elements to produce a product (or service) for a particular market segment. Swatch did this by putting its innovative new clockworks inside a long series of uniquely designed band-case-face configurations, producing many "different" watches for different customer segments from a common base. The true innovation was in the clockworks. That innovation was leveraged in the marketplace by means of platform derivatives. Black & Decker did the same back in the early 1970s. In a classic case of platform innovation, Black & Decker very deliberately created a power tool platform—an electric motor and controls—on which it could base dozens of consumer power tools: electric drills, sanders, saws, grinders, and others. Thanks to that common platform and the cost advantage it conferred, Black & Decker was able to gain leadership in many consumer power tool markets. At the same time it was able to reduce complexity in its operations. Instead of having to manufacture and stock unique motors, components, and switches for every one of its many power tools, the

FIGURE 5-3

Addressing Many Market Segments with a Common Platform

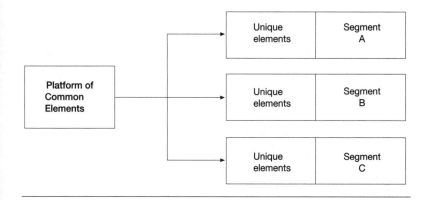

company could accomplish its goals using a single assembly program and common set of components. Costs and components were reduced by orders of magnitude.[6]

The SMH and Black & Decker examples are presented to underscore the value—in some cases—of focusing innovative thinking on platforms instead of on single products and services. What product or service platforms does your company use today? Are promising ideas conceived as single products or services or as platforms capable of supporting many different product or service families? If you are not using a platform approach, think of how a single platform could help you reduce costs and increase variety.

Summing Up

This chapter examined the final phase of the innovation process: moving ideas to the market. In this phase companies must develop a rational approach for rejecting some of the ideas developed earlier and moving others forward toward eventual commercialization. The idea funnel and stage-gate systems were described.

The funnel is not a method but a conceptual framework for understanding what must go on as innovative ideas are moved toward commercialization. By degrees and through rational processes, many ideas are reduced to the most commercially promising few.

The stage-gate system is an alternating series of development stages and assessment "gates" that aims for early elimination of weak ideas and faster time-to-market for potential winners. These stages and gates control events from the birth of an idea all the way to commercialization.

The chapter also discussed the financial tools that become important as an innovative idea moves closer to commercialization. Two assessment methods were described:

- **Breakeven analysis:** A quantitative measure of how many units will have to be sold at a given net price, assuming fixed and variable costs, for the organization to break even.

- **Discounted cash flow (DCF) analysis:** A method for determining the monetary value of a commercialized idea over a particular span of time based on time-value-of-money concepts. The effectiveness of this methodology was shown to be only as good as the assumptions used.

Finally, the chapter introduced the concept of the product platform. Extending innovation through product platforms gives the innovator low-cost opportunities to customize products for different market segments.

6

Creativity and Creative Groups

Two Keys to Innovation

Key Topics Covered in This Chapter

- *Myths about creativity*

- *The components of individual creativity: expertise, flexible and imaginative thinking, and motivation*

- *Characteristics of creative groups*

- *The effect of time pressure on creativity*

PREVIOUS CHAPTERS of this book focused on the front end of the innovative process: idea generation, opportunity recognition, and the processes that companies use to choose among many innovative ideas and move them toward commercialization. Very little was said, however, about the creativity from which innovations emerge, or about the things that managers can do to encourage creativity among individuals and teams. We turn to these topics here and in the succeeding chapter. But first, let's look at some popular misconceptions about creativity.

Myths About Creativity

Quite a bit of research has been done on creativity over the years. This research indicates various misconceptions that limit our ability to effectively manage it:

1. **The smarter you are, the more creative you are.** Reality: Intelligence correlates with creativity only to a point. Once you have enough intelligence to do your job, the correlation no longer holds. That is, above a fairly modest threshold—an IQ of about 120—there is no correlation between intelligence and creativity. As we will see later, there is no valid profile for the creative person, nor is there a test for determining a person's creative powers. So be careful about using IQ tests, grade point averages, and similar measures as you screen the people you look to for creative thinking.

2. **The young are more creative than the old.** Reality: Age is not a clear predictor of creative potential. Research shows that it usually takes seven to ten years to build up deep expertise in a given field—the kind of expertise that enables you to perceive patterns of order or meaning that are invisible to the novice. Thus, in the business world, the necessary creativity can be found in an adult of any age. At the same time, however, expertise can inhibit creativity: Experts sometimes find it difficult to see or think outside established patterns. So when you think about staffing R&D or product development teams, think about balancing them with veterans and newcomers. The veterans have deep expertise; the minds of newcomers are not contaminated by conventional thinking.

3. **Creativity is reserved for the few—the flamboyant risk takers.** Reality: A willingness to take calculated risks and the ability to think in untraditional ways do play roles in creativity. But that doesn't mean you have to be a bungee jumper to be creative. It doesn't mean that you have to be markedly different from everyone else. Nor does it mean that creativity is restricted to high-risk endeavors.

4. **Creativity is a solitary act.** Reality: A high percentage of the world's most important inventions are products of collaboration among groups of people with complementary skills. Given this fact, a smart manager will look for ways of bringing people with complementary skills together: in forums, brown-bag lunches, workshops, and brainstorming teams.

5. **You can't manage creativity.** Reality: Granted, you can never know in advance who will be involved in a creative act, what that act will be, or precisely when or how it will occur. Nevertheless, a manager can create the conditions that make creativity more likely to occur. We've mentioned two in the preceding paragraphs, and others (rewards, resources, structures, etc.) in earlier chapters. Management can make a difference!

Three Components of Individual Creativity

The myths we've just listed certainly cast doubt on the ability of managers to hire the right people and to create environments in which creative behavior can flourish. But these myths do not hold water. So it's best to put them on the shelf and consider what creativity is and the components that make it possible.

Creativity is not a state of mind nor a form of personal "wiring." Instead, *creativity* is a process of developing and expressing novel ideas for solving problems or satisfying needs. Thus, creativity is not so much a talent as it is a goal-oriented process for producing innovations. Managers would find their jobs easier if they could identify this goal-oriented process in the people they hire and assign for particular tasks. Unfortunately, there is no valid profile for these people, nor is there a test for determining a person's creative powers. As researcher Albert Shapiro once put it, "Despite several decades of research effort on creativity and highly creative individuals, there is as yet no profile or test that reliably predicts who will be highly creative in the future."[1]

If an individual's creative behavior cannot be predicted, the materials from which creative behavior emerge have been identified. As described by Teresa Amabile, creativity has three components: expertise, creative-thinking skills, and motivation (figure 6-1). Expertise is technical, procedural, and intellectual knowledge. Creative-thinking skills are defined as the ways in which people approach problems. According to Amabile, creative-thinking skills are often a function of personality and work style. "The pharmaceutical scientist," she writes, "will be more creative if her personality is such that she feels comfortable disagreeing with others."[2] It will also help if her work style is one that doggedly pursues solutions even in the face of disappointing setbacks.

Motivation may be extrinsic or intrinsic, according to Amabile. Extrinsic motivation is induced from the outside through means such as bonuses and promotions. Her research shows that intrinsic motivation—that is, motivation fired by an internal passion or interest—has a greater impact on creativity.

A manager can influence the three components of creativity just described through workplace practices and conditions. Here are the ones that appear to matter most:

FIGURE 6-1

The Three Components of Creativity

Within every individual, creativity is a function of three components: expertise, creative-thinking skills, and motivation. Can managers influence these components? The answer is an emphatic yes—for better or for worse—through workplace practices and conditions.

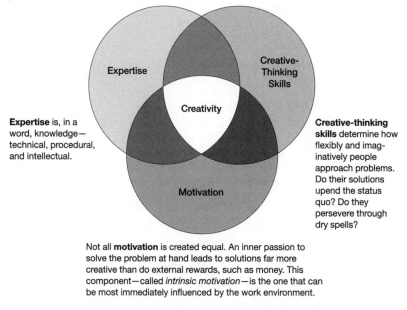

Expertise is, in a word, knowledge— technical, procedural, and intellectual.

Creative-thinking skills determine how flexibly and imaginatively people approach problems. Do their solutions upend the status quo? Do they persevere through dry spells?

Not all **motivation** is created equal. An inner passion to solve the problem at hand leads to solutions far more creative than do external rewards, such as money. This component—called *intrinsic motivation*—is the one that can be most immediately influenced by the work environment.

Source: Teresa M. Amabile, "How to Kill Creativity," *Harvard Business Review,* September–October 1998, 77–87.

- **Getting the right match.** Matching the right people with the right assignments is the simplest and most effective approach to enhancing individual creativity. Effective matching is achieved when managers assign people to jobs that make the most of their expertise, their creative-thinking skills, and their intrinsic motivations.

- **Giving freedom.** Amabile suggests that managers be specific about ends, but leave the means to employees. Doing so will make them more creative. So instead of saying "Do this, and then do that," say "This is our goal; think about the best way to get us there."

- **Providing sufficient time and resources.** People are unlikely to be at their creative best when deadlines are arbitrary or impossible to meet. The same happens when people feel that they lack the resources to do the job well.

Put these three components together, and you will have improved the prospects of generating creative behavior.

Characteristics of Creative Groups

Although creativity is often an individual act, many innovations are products of creative groups. The transistor developed by scientists at Bell Labs is just one example. Many of the breakthroughs achieved by Edison and Eastman were likewise products of those two recognized inventors and the various technicians and engineers who worked with them. Groups can often achieve greater creative output than individuals working alone because they bring a greater sum of competencies, insights, and energy to the effort. But in order to reap this greater output, groups must have the right composition of thinking styles and technical skills. The "right" composition, in most cases, means a diversity of thinking styles and skills. That diversity has several benefits:

- Individual differences can produce a creative friction that sparks new ideas.

- Diversity of thought and perspective is a safeguard against *groupthink*—that is, the tendency of individual thought to converge for social reasons around a particular point of view.

- Diversity of thought and skills gives good ideas more opportunities to develop.

Thus, managers need to consider how work groups are staffed and how they communicate.

The creative group exhibits paradoxical characteristics. It shows tendencies of thought and action that we'd assume to be mutually exclusive or contradictory. For example, to do its best work, a group needs deep knowledge of the subjects relevant to the problem it's trying to solve, and a mastery of the processes involved. But at the same time, the group needs fresh perspectives that are unencumbered by the prevailing wisdom or established ways of doing things. Often called a "beginner's mind," this is the perspective of a newcomer: someone who is curious, even playful, and willing to ask anything—no matter how naive the question may seem—because he doesn't know what he doesn't know. Thus, bringing together contradictory characteristics can catalyze new ideas.

Table 6-1 describes a number of seemingly contradictory characteristics that a group must have to maximize its creative potential. Many people mistakenly assume that creativity is a function of only the elements in the left column of the table: the beginner's mind, freedom, play, and improvisation. But a blend of the left *and* the right columns is needed. This paradoxical combination is confusing and disturbing to managers who have a need for order and linear activity. Accepting it is the first step toward success.

TABLE 6-1

The Paradoxical Characteristics of Creative Groups

Beginner's Mind	A team needs fresh, inexperienced perspectives as well as skilled expertise. Bringing in outsiders is often a useful way to provide the necessary balance of perspective.	**Experience**
Freedom	Your team must work within the confines of real business needs—and in alignment with your company's strategy. But it also needs latitude—some degree of freedom to determine *how* it will achieve the strategy and address the business needs.	**Discipline**
Play	Creativity thrives on playfulness, but business must be conducted professionally. Provide time and space for play, but clarify the appropriate times and places.	**Professionalism**
Improvisation	Plan your project carefully, but remember that projects do not always go as planned. Encourage team members to look for ways to turn unexpected events into opportunities. Keep plans flexible enough to incorporate new or improved ideas.	**Planning**

Source: HMM Managing for Creativity and Innovation.

Divergent and Convergent Thinking

Group creativity is also enhanced when both divergent and convergent thinking are at work. The creative process begins with *divergent thinking*—a breaking away from familiar or established ways of seeing and doing. Divergent thinking has a broad focus. This seems intuitively obvious. If we continually observe an object from the same vantage point and in the same lighting conditions, we are bound to have the same impression of that object. Change the lighting or the viewing angle, however, and perceptions may change. They will become more complete—more nuanced. For example, if you look at the full moon through a small telescope, you will always see a flat, meteor-pocked surface. Look at it again a week or so later and you'll see something very different. Thanks to the contrast created by sunlight and darkness, you will now see rugged mountains, gaping crevices, and deep craters that were impossible to see before.

Seeing things from an unfamiliar perspective makes it possible to develop insights and new ideas. But are those insights valuable? That's what *convergent thinking* attempts to answer. It helps to channel the results of divergent thinking into concrete products and services. As new ideas generated by divergent thinking are communicated to others, they are evaluated to determine which ideas are genuinely novel and worth pursuing. Thus convergent thinking is one of the benefits of group work. Without it, the creative person working alone could easily pursue an idea that eats up time and resources and leads to nothing of value.

In moving from divergent to convergent thinking, a team stops emphasizing what is novel and starts emphasizing what is useful. Convergence sets limits and narrows the field of solutions within a given set of constraints. How do you determine those constraints? The culture, mission, priorities, and high-level concept of your company and project all contribute to the answer. They help you rule out options that lie beyond the scope of your project.

Here are some questions your team might ask as it applies convergent thinking to a range of possible solutions:

- Which functions are essential (from the customer's point of view) and which are only "nice to have"?

- What criteria are determined by the company's values? For example, Fisher-Price groups insist that any toys developed be "Mom-friendly," since most toys are purchased by mothers.

- What are the cost constraints?

- What are the size or shape constraints?

- Within what time must the project be completed?

- In what ways must the product or service be compatible with existing products or services?

Tips for Improving Convergent Thinking

Work groups are often tempted to converge quickly on what appears to be a single best solution and to mute any dissent. It's the team leader or manager's job to prevent both. Consider these suggestions:

- Insist on an incubation period during which people can experiment with the various options. Some options don't seem so promising after people have thought about them for a week or two.

- Appoint an official devil's advocate to challenge all assumptions associated with the group's favored options.

- Ensure that dissent is tolerated and protected and that dissenters have the freedom to voice contrary views. Otherwise, groupthink may take control of future decisions.

Diverse Thinking Styles

Beyond divergent and convergent thinking, a group benefits when its members approach their work with different preferred thinking styles and when they bring a variety of skills to a common effort.

Let's start with thinking styles. A *thinking style* is the unconscious way a person looks at and interacts with the world. When faced with a problem or dilemma, a person will usually approach it through a preferred thought style. Although each style has particular advantages, no one style is better than another.

There are a number of different ways of describing how people think and make decisions. For example, the Myers-Briggs Type Indicator breaks down thinking preferences into four categories, with two opposite tendencies in each category:

1. **Extravert–Introvert.** Extraverted people look to other people as the primary means of processing information. As they get ideas or grapple with problems, they quickly bring them to the attention of others for feedback. Introverted people tend to process information internally first before presenting the results to others.

2. **Sensing–Intuitive.** Sensing people tend to prefer hard data and concrete facts—information that is closely tied to the five senses. Intuitive people are more comfortable with ideas and concepts, with the "big picture."

3. **Thinking–Feeling.** Thinking people prefer logical processes and orderly ways of approaching problems. Feeling people are more attuned to emotional cues; they are more likely to make decisions based on the values or relationships involved.

4. **Judging–Perceiving.** Judging people tend to prefer closure—they like having all the loose ends tied up. By contrast, perceiving people like things more open; they tend to be more comfortable with ambiguity and often want to collect still more data before reaching a decision.

Don't get hung up on the actual word used to describe a particular tendency. Everyone exhibits some aspect of all eight styles, but in varying degrees. For example, a feeling person is not incapable of logical thought—rather, his or her thinking about a decision tends to be guided by the emotional impact of that decision on key relationships.

Well-balanced work groups include representatives of these different preferred thinking styles. How well balanced are your work groups?

Diversity of Skills

Once you've assessed how the thinking styles of your group members complement (or duplicate) each other, you'll have a pretty good feel for whether any gaps exist. It's then time to survey the skills represented on the team. If the team lacks vital technical skills or expertise, it will have trouble developing the ideas it generates. For example, when Thomas Edison began thinking about the prospect of producing the incandescent electric lamp, he knew that he would have to do lots of experimenting with designs and materials. So he created a team that included technicians with machining, laboratory, and glassblowing skills. Their skills made it possible for Edison to test hundreds of filament materials in rapid succession. Eventually, a vacuum bulb containing a carbonized cotton filament proved serviceable. But more experiments with materials were needed before his idea could be commercialized. The technical skill set he assembled made that possible.

In some cases, you may have to look outside your company—or industry—to find the know-how you need. For example, when engineers at a ceramics manufacturer experienced problems getting ceramics to release from their molds, they realized that their problem had to do with quick-freezing, not with ceramics. So instead of seeking out other ceramics experts, they turned to food industry experts, who had special knowledge of quick-freezing.

Generally, you know that it's time to look outward for solutions when a team has been working for a long time on a problem with no solution in sight. The same applies when team members always agree or always disagree on what should be done.

Tips for Filling Team Gaps

As you seek a diverse set of skills and knowledge, keep these tips in mind.

- Look for people whose intellectual perspectives complement—but don't duplicate—your own preferred styles and skills and those of your group.

- Look for a balance of expertise and personal characteristics (such as initiative, ability to get along with others, etc.) in each new hire.

- Look for people who can work across functional boundaries.

- When you specify hiring criteria, put a premium on finding the skills that the group currently lacks. Don't simply list a standard set of skills.

- Explore nontraditional hiring channels—that is, channels other than those used by your company's human resources department.

- Consider adding a customer or outside professional to the group. Either will bring a much different perspective. Xerox engineers, for example, brought in anthropologists to help them design more user-friendly copiers.

Remember too that if your goal is to create change within the group, hiring one person who has a different perspective is insufficient. A lone hire with a different outlook soon feels isolated and ineffective. For different thinking styles to make a difference, two things must happen: You must hire a critical mass of these people, and they must be thoroughly integrated into the team.

Handling Conflict in Groups

Although diversity of thinking and skills is valuable, it's not without hazards. Different thinking styles do not produce unbroken harmony— nor would you want it. Expect disagreement and clashes. The manager's job is to make conflict creative.

For creative conflict to work, team members must listen to each other, be willing to understand different viewpoints, and question each other's assumptions. At the same time, managers must prevent that conflict from becoming personal or from going underground where resentment can simmer. The best antidote to destructive conflict is a set of group norms for dealing with it.

What should your group's operating norms be? That depends on the purpose of the group and the personalities of its members. Just be sure that they are clear and concise. Here are a few examples:

- Every group member should show respect to others.

- Everyone should make a commitment to active listening.

- Everyone has a right to disagree and an obligation to challenge others' assumptions.

- Everyone will have an opportunity to speak.

- Conflicting views are an important source of learning.

- Ideas and assumptions may be attacked but individuals may not.

- Calculated risk taking is good.

- Failures should be acknowledged and examined for their lessons.

- Playful attitudes are welcomed.

- Successes will be celebrated as a group.

Whatever norms your group adopts, make sure that all members have a hand in creating them—and that everyone is willing to abide by them.

Three Steps for Handling Creative Conflict

Even with consensus on norms of behavior, conflict is a fact of life in groups. The following three steps will help you turn that conflict into a creative asset.

1. **Create a climate that makes people willing to discuss difficult issues.** Help your team understand the concept of "the moose on the table" (the big issue or problem that is impeding progress but that no one wants to discuss). Make it clear that you want the tough issues aired and that anyone can point out a moose.

2. **Facilitate the discussion.** How do you deal with a moose once it has been identified? Use the following guidelines:

   a. Stop whatever you are doing and acknowledge the issue, even if only one person sees it.

   b. Refer back to group norms on how people have agreed to treat each other.

   c. Encourage the person who identified the moose to be specific.

   d. Keep the discussion impersonal. The point is not to assign blame—discuss *what* is impeding progress, not *who*.

   If the issue involves someone's behavior, encourage the person who identified the problem to explain how the behavior affects him or her, rather than to make assumptions about the motivation behind the behavior. For example, if someone is not completing work when promised, you might say, "When your work is not completed on time, the group is unable to meet deadlines," not, "I know you are not really excited about this product."

   If someone is not providing necessary leadership, you might say, "When you don't provide us with direction, we spend a lot of time trying to second-guess you, and that makes us feel unproductive," not, "You don't seem to have any idea what we should be doing on this project."

3. **Move toward closure by discussing what can be done.** Leave
with some concrete suggestions for improvement, if not a solution to the problem.

If the subject is too sensitive and discussions are going
nowhere, consider adjourning your meeting until a specified
later date so that people can cool down. Or, consider bringing
in a facilitator.

Time Pressure and Creativity

Time is one of the things that every creative individual and creative
team must have to achieve anything worthwhile. But how much
time do they need? How much time should managers give them?
These are important questions for managers as they attempt to meet
organizational goals with limited resources.

Academics have studied the time pressure–creativity connection
for a long time. In general, these studies point to a curvilinear relationship between the two—that is, to a certain point, pressure helps.
But beyond that point, pressure has a negative impact. Teresa Amabile, Constance Hadley, and Steven Kramer continued that research,
reaching some eye-opening conclusions. They point to instances
where ingenuity flourishes under extreme time pressure—just as
managers have always believed (or hoped). They point, for example,
to a NASA team that within hours came up with a crude but effective fix for the air filtration system aboard Apollo 13—a creative solution that saved the mission and its crew. On the other hand, they
point to the Bell Labs teams that felt no such pressure, but which
nevertheless created the transistor and the laser.

After studying over nine thousand daily diary entries of people
engaged in projects demanding high levels of creativity, they concluded that time pressure usually kills creativity. "Our study indicates
that the more time pressure people feel on a given day," they write,
"the less likely they will be to think creatively."[3]

That's bad news for companies and managers, but not entirely bad.
These researchers noted that time pressure affects creativity in different

FIGURE 6 - 2

The Time Pressure/Creativity Matrix

Our study suggests that time pressure affects creativity in different ways depending on whether the environment allows people to focus on their work, conveys a sense of meaningful urgency about the tasks at hand, or stimulates or undermines creative thinking in other ways.

	Time Pressure	
	Low	High
High — Likelihood of Creative Thinking	Creative thinking under low time pressure is more likely when people feel as if they are **on an expedition**. They: • show creative thinking that is more oriented toward generating or exploring ideas than identifying problems. • tend to collaborate with one person rather than with a group.	Creative thinking under extreme time pressure is more likely when people feel as if they are **on a mission**. They: • can focus on one activity for a significant part of the day because they are undisturbed or protected. • believe that they are doing important work and report feeling positively challenged by and involved in the work. • show creative thinking that is equally oriented toward identifying problems and generating or exploring ideas.
Low	Creative thinking under low time pressure is unlikely when people feel as if they are **on autopilot**. They: • receive little encouragement from senior management to be creative. • tend to have more meetings and discussions with groups rather than with individuals. • engage in less collaborative work overall.	Creative thinking under extreme time pressure is unlikely when people feel as if they are **on a treadmill**. They: • feel distracted. • experience a highly fragmented workday, with many different activities. • don't get the sense that the work they are doing is important. • feel more pressed for time than when they are "on a mission" even though they work the same number of hours. • tend to have more meetings and discussions with groups rather than with individuals. • experience lots of last-minute changes in their plans and schedules.

Source: Teresa M. Amabile, Constance N. Hadley, and Steven J. Kramer, "Creativity Under the Gun," *Harvard Business Review,* August 2002, 56.

ways depending on whether the environment allows people to focus on their work, conveys a sense of meaningful urgency about their tasks, or stimulates or undermines creativity in other ways. For example, time pressure is not a creativity killer when people feel that they are on a mission, which is what the NASA crew undoubtedly felt.

To help managers understand when and how time pressure affects creativity, we've reproduced the four-quadrant matrix developed by Amabile and her associates (figure 6-2).

Six Steps for Increasing Your Own Creativity

This chapter has indicated how you, as a manager, can help employees and groups be more creative. But what about you? How can you increase your own creativity? Here are six suggested steps:

1. **Strive for alignment.** Make sure that the goals of the organization you work for are consonant with your most cherished values. Instead of considering jobs at which you excel, think instead about jobs that match your deeply embedded life interests.

2. **Pursue some self-initiated activity.** Choose projects where your intrinsic motivation is high. If you have always loved graphic design, try to determine why the packaging for one of your company's products leaves customers cold.

3. **Take advantage of unofficial activity.** The absence of official status may create a safe haven for nurturing an idea until it is strong enough to overcome resistance.

4. **Be open to serendipity.** Develop a bias toward action and toward trying new ideas. For instance, if an accident or failure occurs while you're prototyping a new LCD screen, don't dismiss it too quickly. Study it for the learning opportunity that may lie within. Each day, write down what surprised you and how you surprised others.

5. **Diversify your stimuli.** Intellectual cross–pollination gets you thinking in new directions. Develop cross-functional skills: Rotate into every job you are capable of doing. Get to know people who spark your imagination. Become a lifelong learner: Take classes not related to your work. Bring your insights from outside interests or activities to bear on your workplace challenges.

6. **Create opportunities for informal communication.** Take advantage of unanticipated opportunities to exchange ideas with colleagues. Creative thought often happens during spontaneous interactions between individuals. Such interactions, however, are only useful if real communication occurs. You must find ways to encourage and facilitate communication that is appropriate for the creative environment.

Summing Up

This chapter addressed the subject of creativity in individuals and teams. It began by exploring several myths about creativity. Contrary to conventional thinking:

- Intelligence and creativity are only weakly correlated.

- Age is not a clear predictor of creative potential.

- Calculated risk taking and the ability to think in untraditional ways play roles in creativity.

- A high percentage of important inventions are products of collaborative effort.

- Managers can make a difference in creativity output—they can create the conditions that make creativity more likely to occur.

Next, creativity was shown to have three components that you should bring to your organization's problems:

1. Expertise in terms of technical, procedural, and intellectual knowledge

2. Creative thinking skills, as revealed by how people approach problems

3. Motivation: intrinsic and extrinsic

Organizations have found that innovation is generally a function of collaboration between individuals working within groups. With that in mind, the chapter identified the characteristics of creative groups. Groups must have the right composition of thinking styles and technical skills. The "right" composition, in most cases, means a diversity of thinking styles and skills. It also means bring together some paradoxical characteristics:

• The "beginner's mind" and experience

• Freedom and discipline

• Play and professionalism

• Improvisation and planning

Group creativity is also enhanced when both divergent and convergent thinking are at work. Divergent thinking is a breaking away from familiar or established ways. Convergent thinking attempts to find the value of creative insights.

The chapter also examined the issue of time pressure, which affects both individual and group creativity. Is time pressure a good thing or a bad thing? Much research has been done on this issue, and the latest points to the conclusion that time pressure affects creativity in different ways depending on whether the environment allows people to focus on their work, conveys a sense of meaningful urgency about their tasks, or stimulates or undermines creativity in other ways.

Finally, how can you be more creative? Six steps were offered:

1. Strive for alignment.

2. Pursue some self-initiated activity.

3. Take advantage of unofficial activity.

4. Be open to serendipity.

5. Diversify your stimuli.

6. Create opportunities for informal communication.

Enhancing Creativity

Enriching the Organization and Workplace

Key Topics Covered in This Chapter

- *Six ways to organizational enrichment*

- *How to enrich the physical workplace*

HIRING CREATIVE PEOPLE and grouping them into well-crafted teams, as described in chapter 6, is an essential first step toward producing greater creativity and useful innovation. The second step is more difficult and requires support at the highest levels. It involves making the organization and the physical workplace more supportive of creativity and innovation.

Organizational Enrichment

Even if you have put together a really hot team of creative people, that team will produce disappointing results if it's condemned to operate within an organization that's unfriendly to new ideas. This was precisely what people in Xerox Corporation's Palo Alto Research Center (PARC) experienced during the late 1970s and early 1980s. PARC was (and remains) a cornucopia of innovative thinking. Its brainy scientists and engineers had conjured up many of the technologies that would eventually power the emerging era of desktop computing: ethernet connectivity, the mouse, and a user-friendly operating system. Xerox management, however, was not receptive to those innovations, which were not going to produce financial returns in the time frame required by the company. Many of PARC's innovations found their way into personal computers developed by Apple.

Hewlett-Packard innovators encountered a different but equally frustrating experience around 1990. The open, decentralized organization created by founders William Hewlett and David Packard had been highly encouraging to innovators and had put the company at the forefront of many emerging product categories. But the retirement of the founders, new management, and enormous business growth resulted in a more centralized and bureaucratic organization. People with innovative ideas now found that they had to gain approvals from many layers of committees before they could move forward. The result was a marked slowdown in new product introductions and plummeting profits. Thankfully, the company's aging founders intervened, broke up the bureaucratic tangle, and returned HP to its characteristic idea-friendly ways. A huge leap in new product introductions followed—as did profits.

The Xerox and Hewlett-Packard examples underscore the impact of organizational practices on creativity and the innovations it produces. Table 7-1 lists the characteristics that support and encourage creativity and innovation. The converse of these characteristics actually discourages both. Consider these characteristics and how your company or your operating unit stands relative to them. Is it strong? Is it weak? If it's weak, what can be done to change the situation? Let's consider each characteristic in detail.

TABLE 7-1

Checklist of Organizational Characteristics That Support Creativity and Innovation

| | My Company's Rating | |
Characteristic	Strong	Weak
Risk taking is acceptable to management.		
New ideas and new ways of doing things are welcomed.		
Information is free flowing—and not controlled by managers.		
Employees have access to knowledge sources: customers, benchmarking partners, the scientific community, and so forth.		
Good ideas are supported by executive patrons.		
Innovators are rewarded.		

Risk Taking Is Acceptable to Management

Risk aversion is normal and healthy. But progress and risk are inseparable companions. You cannot have one without the other. "You have to promote risk-taking," Esther Dyson told readers of *Harvard Business Review.* "Be open to experimentation and philosophical about things that go wrong. My motto is, 'Always make a new mistake.' There's no shame in making a mistake. But then learn from it and don't make the same one again. Everything I've learned, I've learned by making mistakes." [1]

Management must recognize the risk/reward relationship and find organizational mechanisms for handling it. And it must communicate a clear understanding that reasonable risks are acceptable, since they are the handmaidens of progress. On the innovative front, two methods are available for dealing with risk: diversification and cheap failures. They can and should be used in concert.

Diversification allows companies to spread risk over many rolls of the dice, as opposed to betting the company on a single roll. For example, if one hundred individuals are taking calculated risks on innovative ideas, experience generally shows that some will be total failures, others will roughly break even, and some others will be very successful, producing a net positive outcome for all one hundred ventures. Because one can never know in advance which ideas will be winners and which will be losers, having a diversified "portfolio" of ideas in play makes sense.

Cheap failure is the second method for dealing with risk. A cheap failure is a project or experiment that is terminated with the least possible outlay of resources—just enough to tell managers that "This isn't going to work." A direct analogy to cheap failure is found in card playing. A smart card player knows that he can't expect to win if he stays out of play, so he puts down his ante and waits for his cards. If those cards are strong, he'll stay in the game, matching or raising other bids. As he draws more cards, the player will decide whether staying in a particular game is worth the cost. His goal is to get out of losing games as quickly and cheaply as possible. Smart companies treat ideas in the same way. They back promising ideas with small budgets and look for ways to test them with the least input of resources. Like card players, they quickly fold when they recognize that they have a weak hand. Conversely, they increase backing for strong ideas.

New Ideas and New Ways of Doing Things Are Welcomed

The worst environment for creativity is one that is unwelcoming to new ideas. "Why bother to come up with new ideas," people ask, "when management shoots down everything?" Some senior managers are so bound up with the status quo that they have no enthusiasm for anything that's new or different. "We've been successful over the years by doing things this way, so why should we change?" An organization with this attitude is heading for trouble.

In fairness, management is compelled to shoot down good ideas when (1) those ideas lack a strategic fit with the business, or (2) the organization lacks the resources to pursue them. In these cases, however, management has a responsibility to communicate its reasoning to employees.

Beyond welcoming new ideas, the organization should view innovation as a normal part of business—not a special activity practiced by a handful of employees. That's the advice of Craig Wynett, general manager of future growth initiatives at Procter & Gamble. "What we've done to encourage innovation is make it ordinary," says Wynett.

> By that I mean we don't separate it from the rest of our business. Many companies make innovation front page news, and all that special attention has a paradoxical effect. By serving it up as something exotic, you isolate it from what's normal. . . . At P&G, we think of creativity not as a mysterious gift of the talented few but as the everyday task of making non-obvious connections—bringing together things that don't normally go together. . . .
>
> Isolating innovation from mainstream business can produce a dangerous cultural side effect: Creativity and leadership can be perceived as opposites. This artificial disconnect means that innovators often lack the visibility and clout to compete for the resources necessary for success.[2]

Information Is Free Flowing

Information can stimulate thinking, which leads to idea generation. Here's why. As explained earlier in this book, many creative ideas are formed at the intersection of different lines of thought or technology. For example, Harold is working on vehicle steering systems; Maude is an expert in electromechanical applications. When these two communicate and share information, they get an idea for an electronic steering system that hasn't yet been considered.

In hierarchical firms, information is often hoarded as a source of organizational power. Information flows are controlled and channeled through the chain of command. People must demonstrate a "need to know" to have access to certain information. This control impedes the catalytic function of communication and limits opportunities for different pieces of information to intersect and combine in people's minds. For example, if Harold and Maude are not able to communicate directly with one another, their new idea may not form.

Managers can encourage the free flow of information in many ways: through e-mail, the physical co-location of team members, joint work sessions, and regular brown-bag lunches. This topic is explored further in the section "Enriching the Physical Workplace."

Employees Have Access to Knowledge Sources

Just as employees must have free-flowing lines of communication between one another, so too they need access to sources of knowledge—both inside and outside the organization. That knowledge is often the raw material of creative thought.

Some companies have developed elaborate knowledge management systems to capture knowledge, store it, and make it easily available for reuse. These systems help ensure that what was learned by someone in Unit A doesn't have to be learned anew by someone in Unit B. Lee Sage has described DaimlerChrysler's Engineering Books of Knowledge (EBOKs), a knowledge management database containing technical data, lessons learned, and best practices that is made available to the company's engineering community. The purpose of the EBOKs, according to Sage, is to capture the expert knowledge of technical employees and use it to improve engineering productivity, speed new product development, and avoid repeating past mistakes.[3] Consulting and tax accounting companies use knowledge management systems in similar ways.

Another way to help employees tap sources of internal knowledge is through the creation of communities of interest. A *community of interest* is an informal group whose members share an interest in some technology or application. The group might be a dozen engineers from different operating units who share a common interest in adhesive applications. It might be a group of managers interested in benchmarking techniques. Whatever the interest may be, newsletters and periodic meetings held by these communities provide opportunities to share knowledge and spark the imagination.

External knowledge is equally important as a stimulant to innovation. External knowledge invigorates and adds vitality to organizations. Employees access that knowledge when they have opportunities to attend professional and scientific meetings and to visit customers and benchmarking partners, and when outside experts are brought in to share their know-how via lectures and workshops.

One of the classic cases of tapping external sources of knowledge occurred in the early 1980s when Xerox Corporation sent a team of logistics personnel to visit the warehouse of outdoor outfitter L.L. Bean in Freeport, Maine. Xerox had identified picking, packing, and shipping of individual replacement parts and user supplies as a critical bottleneck in its fulfillment operation. To eliminate that bottleneck, it began searching for best-practice know-how. Library research turned up an article identifying L.L. Bean as a company that had mastered the art of quickly and accurately filling small, individual orders of one to three items—just what Xerox was attempting to do without success. Within a short time, a Xerox team was dispatched to Freeport to observe L.L. Bean's methods, which were later adapted successfully to the copier company's fulfillment process.[4]

What sources of external knowledge are your people tapping today? Do they have resources and management encouragement to seek out relevant knowledge?

Good Ideas Are Supported by Executive Patrons

Organizations need people in high places who will champion good ideas and provide them with moral support and protection as they travel the bumpy road toward commercialization. Leifer and colleagues observed a form of executive patronage in each of the radical innovation projects they studied. They concluded, for example, that IBM's silicon germanium computer chip project would not likely have survived without the implicit protection of two senior IBM executives, who over a period of years provided under-the-table resources to keep that project alive. They observed the same at General Electric, where a now-successful digital x-ray technology would have died on the vine had it not been for the backing of two high-placed executives—one being then-CEO Jack Welch.[5]

If you had a great idea, would anyone in senior management have the interest and the courage to act as its patron? Would that person provide protection and resources?

Although executive patronage is often necessary for radical innovation, such support is not always well directed. Senior executives are not necessarily more clairvoyant than other managers, and they sometimes place their bets on the wrong ponies. Motorola's Bill Galvin backed the costly Iridium misadventure. Polaroid's Edwin Land invested heavily in Polarvision, a failed attempt to produce instant movies. And Steve Jobs, who demonstrated great foresight in other areas, lost heavily in his support of NEXT. Nevertheless, research points to executive patronage as an important contributor to radical innovation.

Innovators Are Rewarded

Creativity will not flourish in the absence of a reward system that encourages individuals to stretch beyond the bounds of normal work. Creative energy is quickly dissipated and must be replenished somehow. Rewards serve this purpose.

Rewards can be based on the following:

- **Recognition:** Acknowledging individual or group achievement with a plaque or public announcement

- **Control:** Allowing an individual or group to participate in decision making or giving the individual or group the resources needed to carry out a project

- **Celebration:** For example, acknowledging a successful new-product launch by throwing a party

- **Rejuvenation:** Providing time off or away from the task

As described in chapter 6, motivating rewards can either be intrinsic or extrinsic. An *intrinsic reward* appeals to a person's desire for self-actualization, curiosity, enjoyment, or interest in the work itself. An *extrinsic reward* appeals to a person's desire for attainment distinct from the work itself: a cash bonus, a promotion, or stock options. These two sources of motivation work hand in hand. Especially when the work is not routine, intrinsic motivation can help generate creative thought. Just make sure that the rewards or incentives you establish don't become more important than the work itself, thereby undermining team members' intrinsic motivation. At the same time, don't underestimate the power of money, recognition, or other incentives to bolster a group member's self-esteem and thus enhance his or her intrinsic motivation.

It's highly unlikely that you'll have the authority to create a compensation plan for your team, but there probably are areas where you have the power to tweak the existing system with informal rewards to better suit your team's situation.

Some companies have deliberately shaped their organizational practices and policies to support employee creativity and innovation. St. Paul–based 3M Company is one, and it has a longer history of doing so than just about any other U.S. firm. Long before anyone thought to study or codify the creativity-enhancing characteristics described in this chapter, 3M had woven them into the fabric of its corporate culture (see "The 3M Way to Creativity and Innovation").

As this chapter makes clear, creativity is a function of many things, including how it is managed. For a diagnostic checklist that you can use to evaluate the creativity of your workplace, see Appendix B.

The 3M Way to Creativity and Innovation

3M has evolved from a maker of sandpaper to a manufacturer of hundreds of different products, including adhesives, films, and fiber optics. In almost a century, it has commercialized over fifty thousand products. Its success as an innovator is generally attributed to its corporate culture, which very deliberately fosters creativity by giving employees the freedom to take risks and tinker with new ideas. That culture is a legacy of William L. McKnight (1887–1978).

McKnight joined 3M in 1907 as an assistant bookkeeper but rose rapidly through the ranks, becoming president in 1929 and board chairman in 1949. During his tenure he worked to create a culture that put employees in direct contact with customer problems and that encouraged initiative and innovation. His philosophy was to listen to anyone who proposed an original idea and to let him or her run with that idea through "experimental doodling." As he wrote in 1948:

As our business grows, it becomes increasingly necessary to delegate responsibility and to encourage men and women to exercise their initiative. This requires considerable tolerance. Those men and women to whom we delegate authority and responsibility, if they are good people, are going to want to do their jobs in their own way.

Mistakes will be made. But if a person is essentially right, the mistakes he or she makes are not as serious in the long run as the mistakes management will make if it undertakes to tell those in authority exactly how they must do their jobs. Management that is destructively critical when mistakes are made kills initiative. And it's essential that we have many people with initiative if we are to continue to grow.[6]

Today the company backs up McKnight's management philosophy with a number of creativity-supporting practices. Here are just a few:

- McKnight's notion of experimental doodling is institutionalized into 3M's unofficial "15 Percent Rule," which allows technical and scientific employees to use that percentage of their time to pursue ideas unrelated to their official assignments. The 15 Percent Rule has spawned a number of commercially successful products over the years.

- The work of outstanding technical employees is recognized by admission to the prestigious Carlton Society, which opens its doors to a few remarkable innovators each year. These individuals are chosen by their peers in recognition of their outstanding contributions to new technologies and 3M products.

- Teams that create products that earn $4 million or more in profitable revenues receive the Golden Step award.

- Employees can choose between management and technical career ladders. Not everyone is cut out to be a manager, and not all who are qualified for management want to leave the laboratory.

These organizational features are part of 3M's culture of innovation, and they help account for the company's success in producing new and useful products decade after decade. That culture is changing with new management and a new competitive environment, so there is no guarantee that it will remain a culture of innovation.

Enriching the Physical Workplace

As we've seen, organizational features—culture, if you will—have an effect on the creative output of managers and employees. If the organizational environment doesn't expect, encourage, or honor creativity, it will get exactly what it anticipates—very little. In contrast, organizations that have been wellsprings of creativity over many decades (companies such as 3M, Ciba-Geigy, Corning, Siemens, Sony, Hewlett-Packard, Merck, Motorola, Nokia, and Procter & Gamble) organize and behave as though creativity matters.

Physical surroundings can also have an impact on creativity. Even though space costs are usually second only to people costs, many executives are just awakening to the importance of the physical environment. Like the organizational environment, the physical environment can be engineered in ways that encourage higher creative output. For example, when an environment is filled with many types of stimuli and when it provides physical and electronic links between individuals, it encourages people to see new connections and to think more broadly.

In the late 1990s, a team of researchers at MIT's School of Architecture and Planning—the Space Organization Research Group (SORG)—began looking at the connection between workspace design and work processes. They found that, in general, companies attempt to fit work processes into a fairly standard set of physical surroundings—the warren of office cubicles and conference rooms that most of us inhabit from 9 to 5. These companies allow work processes to be determined by existing spaces, which are essentially fixed. This is like putting the cart before the horse. Work processes need the flexibility to be altered from time to time as objectives vary.

One of SORG's more interesting case studies involved a workspace being developed for a new project team at a Xerox Corporation research center in New York state.[7] There, the space and the work were designed simultaneously and with a high level of coordination. Team members were co-located for easier communication with each other and with the physical equipment that occupied their thoughts and experiments. Lines of movement into, out of, and through the workspace were deliberately laid out to create opportunities for frequent and convenient contact between teammates. Meeting rooms were designed so that physical artifacts in the labs were in sight and physically accessible. Meetings were open to all.

Though the actual outcome of the Xerox case could not be determined during the period of SORG's observation, a small but growing body of research is demonstrating what intuition would tell us—that workspace design and work effectiveness are linked.

Modern management's shift toward less formal, team-based ways of working has forced architects and designers to develop spaces that are more adaptable to work process changes and more supportive of creative and cognitive patterns of work. This is the logic behind BMW's Munich engineering center, known as FIZ.

FIZ, which opened in 1987, is based on the concept of co-location. It brings together in one site everyone concerned with auto product development, including BMW's suppliers. Approximately five thousand researchers, engineers, and technicians currently work in the FIZ, which is designed around a network that links various groups together. The maximum walking distance between any two FIZ occupants is 150 meters. That encourages physical contact and informal communication between the many people who work toward common objectives. DaimlerChrysler attempted something very similar—but on twice the scale—when it built its Technology Center in Auburn Hills, Michigan.

What's the nature of your workplace? Do you work out of a closed office where contacts with other key people are strictly accidental or planned in advance?

What is the physical distance between you and the people with whom you should be interacting and sharing ideas on a regular basis? Organizational researchers have known for a long time that the frequency of communication between coworkers decreases dramatically as the physical distance between them increases. As MIT researcher Tom Allen discovered years ago, "People are more likely to communicate with those who are located nearest to them. Individuals and groups can therefore be positioned in ways that will either promote or inhibit communication."[8] Thus, workspace design and the physical location of project team members have a major impact on the depth of communication and knowledge sharing.

Table 7-2 is a worksheet for inventorying your workspace and generating ideas for improvement. Further tips for making the physical environment more friendly to creativity can be found in "Tips for Improving the Physical Environment."

TABLE 7-2

Enhancing the Creativity of the Physical Workspace

Dimension	Current Condition	Ideas for Improvement
Accessible, casual meeting space		
Physical stimuli (for example, books, videos, art on walls, journals)		
Space for quiet reflection		
Variety of communication tools (for example, whiteboards, bulletin boards, e-mail)		
Employee-only space		
Customer contact space		
Space for individual expression		
Game or relaxation area		

For an interactive version of this worksheet and other relevant tools, visit http://www.elearning.hbsp.org/businesstools.

Source: HMM Managing for Creativity and Innovation.

Tips for Improving the Physical Environment

You may not be able to design your workspace from the ground up, but there are valuable—and relatively inexpensive—steps you can take to enhance your team's physical surroundings. The idea is to encourage the interactions that lead to information sharing and creative ideas.

• Conversations and spontaneous meetings often occur in public areas: mailrooms, kitchens, and around water coolers. So make these spaces into comfortable gathering places where people will linger and share ideas.

• Place beanbag chairs in alcoves to create casual meeting areas.

• Place whiteboards and flip charts in places where people naturally congregate. This will allow them to sketch out their ideas during spontaneous discussions.

• Spread crayons and white paper on conference and lunch room tables to encourage doodling and idea diagramming— two modes of thought that are very different from verbal discussion.

• Institute a weekly brown-bag lunch at which people take turns telling their coworkers about their ideas and soliciting feedback.

• Give teams "war rooms" in which they can meet, plan, post information, and display competing products.

Summing Up

This chapter focused on the institutional factors that promote or stifle creativity. The first of these were organizational. Six approaches to enriching the creativity of the organization were suggested:

1. Acceptance of risk taking

2. Welcoming new ideas and ways of doing things

3. Ensuring a free flow of information

4. Giving employees access to knowledge sources

5. Support of good ideas by executives

6. Rewarding innovators

But the organization of a company isn't everything. The physical workplace can also inhibit or enhance creativity. Drawing on several lines of research, the following practices were suggested:

- Design space and the work processes together.

- Co-locate teams and knowledge sources for easier communication with each other and with the physical equipment that occupies their thoughts and experiments.

- Design the physical space so that contact between teammates is frequent and convenient.

8

What Leaders Must Do

Making a Difference

Key Topics Covered in This Chapter

- *Developing a culture that nurtures creativity and innovation*

- *Establishing the strategic direction within which innovation should take place*

- *Being involved with innovation*

- *Being open but skeptical*

- *Improving the idea-to-commercialization process*

- *Applying portfolio thinking*

- *Putting the right people in charge*

- *Creating an ambidextrous organization*

JUST ABOUT EVERYTHING that gets done in a sizable company with respect to idea generation and development is accomplished by middle-level managers and people below them on the organizational chart. But the senior leadership also has a role to play—in shaping the culture, giving direction, allocating resources, and creating balance between what matters today and in the future. This chapter explains, in broad strokes, what leaders must do to assure that innovation flourishes.

Develop an Innovation-Friendly Culture

The impact of organizational culture on creativity and idea generation was discussed in chapter 7. In the absence of a supportive culture, creativity and innovation are like seedlings planted in arid, rocky soil. They simply won't germinate and grow.

Tushman and O'Reilly point to pre-Gerstner IBM as a culture in which innovation fell on arid soil. It was, in their words, "a culture characterized by an inward focus, extensive procedures for resolving issue through consensus and 'push back,' arrogance bred by previous success, and a sense of entitlement on the part of some employees that guaranteed jobs without a quid pro quo."[1] If those words describe your company's culture, then creativity and innovation are not likely to flourish, and the most innovative people will become discouraged and dispirited. The antidote is cultural change, which is a job for senior leaders, who should ask themselves the following questions:

- Is our current success making us self-satisfied and complacent?

- Are we inwardly focused?

- Do we punish risk takers who fail?

- Are creative people and new ideas unwelcome in this company?

- Are we excessively bureaucratic in how we handle new ideas?

- Do we fail to reward acts of creativity?

If you answered "yes" to any one of these questions, a serious evaluation and adjustment of your organizational culture may be in order.

Unfortunately, cultural change is the most difficult type of change. Top management and a small team of consultants can change the structure of an organization by fiat through reorganization, merger, or divestiture. Change that involves downsizing can also be commanded from the top. But to change an organization's culture, people must be motivated and induced to think and act differently. That's a major shift that takes time and the support of people at every level. In many cases a major crisis is required to get that support. British Airways, Continental Airlines, and IBM each experienced crises in the 1990s, and in each case a combination of immediate peril and strong leadership provided the motivation that employees needed to support cultural change.

This raises an important question: "Do we have to wait for a crisis before change is possible?" No, according to Harvard Business School professor Mike Beer. He believes that change leaders can create legitimate concerns about the current situation and offers the following four approaches for doing so.[2] Collectively, they urge management to challenge complacency.

1. **Use information about the organization's competitive situation to generate discussion with employees about current and prospective problems.** Top management, according to Beer, often fails to understand why employees are not as concerned about innovation, customer service, or costs as they are. Too often this is because management has failed to put employees in

touch with the relevant data. In the absence of data, everything appears to be fine.

2. **Create dialogue on the data.** Providing data is one thing. Creating dialogue on the data is something entirely different and more productive. Dialogue should aim for a joint understanding of company problems. Dialogue is a means by which both managers and employees can inform each other of their assumptions and their diagnoses.

3. **Create opportunities for employees to educate management about the dissatisfactions and problems they experience.** In some cases, top management is out of touch with the weaknesses of the business or emerging threats—things that front-line employees understand through daily experience on the factory floor or in face-to-face dealings with customers. If this is your company's problem, find ways to improve communications between top management and front-line people.

4. **Set high standards and expect people to meet them.** The act of stating high standards creates dissatisfaction with the current level of performance.

Tips for Changing Organizational Culture

- Make sure that all four of these change-ready conditions are present:

    1. Leaders are respected, credible, and effective.

    2. People are dissatisfied with the status quo and feel personally motivated to change.

    3. The organization is nonhierarchical.

    4. People are accustomed to and value collaborative work.

Changing the culture of an organization in the absence of these conditions is extremely difficult. So if your company lacks any one condition, work on it first.

- Mobilize energy and commitment to change through joint diagnosis of business problems. Remember, you can't order energy and commitment the way you would a monthly report, but you can generate energy and commitment if you involve people in the process of identifying problems and solutions. In most cases, they will know more about the problems than you will because they are closer to them.

- Don't try to change everything at once. Unless the entire organization is in crisis, begin with change-ready units far from corporate headquarters, where local managers and their people can run the show and maintain control. Use successful change in those units as test beds from which to spread change gradually to other units.

- Create an appealing and shared vision of the future. People won't buy into the pain and effort of change unless they can see a future state that is tangibly better—and better for them—than the one they have at the moment. Successful change leaders form such a vision and communicate it in compelling terms.

- Support change from the top, but leave the thinking and doing to unit leaders and those most affected by the change. Above all, don't put human resources personnel in charge. Give the responsibility to unit line managers.

- Celebrate milestones. Cultural change is a long journey with many milestones. Celebrating the achievement of each milestone recognizes progress and reenergizes commitment.

Establish Strategic Direction

Setting strategic direction is another responsibility of senior leaders. If creative people don't understand where the company is headed, they are likely to generate and pursue ideas that don't fit, that eat up resources, and that will eventually be rejected prior to commercialization. That costs money and dissipates the energy of idea generators.

Since both creative energy and money are scarce commodities, it makes sense to encourage idea generation within boundaries defined by company strategy. For example, if you're a direct-mail apparel merchandiser, you may wish to encourage ideas that fall within the boundaries of "providing better linkages with our customers and providing fast and accurate order fulfillment." Within those strategy-related boundaries, new ideas for improving customer intelligence, order processing, and logistics would be welcomed. Set the boundaries right and your company's creative energies will naturally focus themselves in areas with the greatest payoff potential.

The effect of setting strategic direction and establishing boundaries for ideas will be much greater if you do three things:

1. **Communicate.** This might seem obvious, but it's rare to find an organization whose employees can clearly articulate company strategy—particularly employees at lower levels. "I just do my job," they'll say. So communicate strategic direction clearly and often.

2. **Hire right.** Every innovative organization has to see selection and recruitment as a critical issue and not a distraction to getting the everyday work done. Use every hiring opportunity to populate the organization with people whose special training, experience, or personal interests are aligned with the strategic direction of the company.

3. **Align resources with strategy.** People follow the money. Once they see ideas that fall within stated boundaries being funded for development, they'll channel their creative energies in that direction. Senior management should also review its existing development projects and pull the plug on those that no longer enjoy a strategic fit.

Be Involved with Innovation

Some of the best and most successful executives were happiest and most effective when they were down in the R&D lab rubbing elbows with bench scientists and technicians. Bill Hewlett, David Packard, and Motorola's Bob Galvin fit this description. So does Bill Gates today. It's impossible to make a direct correlation between the R&D involvement of these executives and the success of their organizations, but we know intuitively that leaders cannot make good decisions if they operate in a vacuum or think of innovation as a mysterious force. They must understand the technical issues facing their organizations and the portfolio of ideas and projects that are in the pipeline at any given time. Hewlett, Packard, Galvin, and Gates all did this.

More important, leaders must assess the individual innovators who drop new ideas into their laps from time to time.

- Who are these people anyway?

- Do they have good judgment?

- Do they understand customers and the way customers see the world?

- Are they cautious optimists or hucksters who'll give you all the reasons to say "yes" but conceal every reason to say "no"?

These questions cannot be answered if decision makers and innovators operate in orbits that never intersect. The best way to answer these questions and provide leadership for innovation is to be personally involved. So visit the research center on a regular basis. Have lunch with project teams. Get to know key people one-on-one. Try to understand the technical hurdles that stand between appealing ideas and their commercialization.

Research by Harvard Business School Dean of the Faculty and George F. Baker Professor of Administration Kim Clark and professor Steven Wheelwright indicates that few senior leaders follow that advice.[3] Their involvement in development projects typically begins when projects are nearing the end of the development pipeline—in the pilot or manufacturing ramp-up stages. This is too late in the game to affect the shape or direction of these projects, and reduces the role of senior leadership to saying "Kill" or "Go."

Organizational leaders should do just the opposite. They should be visible and personally involved in the early stages of the innovation process. Doing so has four important benefits:

1. It sends a powerful signal to employees that innovation matters.

2. It provides senior management with opportunities to articulate the strategic direction of the firm and the boundaries within which innovation should be pursued.

3. It gives senior management a direct hand in the design of products and services that will define the company in the future.

4. It educates leaders on technical and market issues and prepares them to act as recognizers and patrons of good ideas.

So if you are a senior manager, ask yourself these questions:

- Am I spending only a very small percentage of my time on the innovation front?

- Am I leaving early design decisions to low-level personnel who may not understand the big picture of our business?

- Have I become insulated from the technological issues shaping our business?

- Is my involvement so late in the process that my only interest is in whether a project will clear financial hurdles?

If you answered "yes" to any of these questions, you need to reconsider how you're spending your time. Innovation and R&D are the crucibles within which the future company is being formed today— you need to be there.

Be Open but Skeptical

Close contact with innovation and R&D will test your judgment. Some people will "pitch" their ideas to you and look for support and resources.

Approach these encounters with a balance of open-mindedness and scientific skepticism. That means two things: (1) demonstrating an interest in new ideas, even when they challenge the company's current products and ways of operating, and (2) simultaneously maintaining scientific skepticism. The two are not incompatible; they can be achieved through honest dialogue, as in this example:

Idea Generator: I think that this new service would really sell.

Leader: Really? To whom?

Idea Generator: Well, to our current customers and to others.

Leader: Why do you believe that? What problem would the service solve for them?

Idea Generator: It would save them lots of time.

Leader: How much time would it actually save them? And how much would they be willing to pay for that benefit?

Idea Generator: I can't answer either of those questions yet.

Leader: Then give some thought to how we can find the answers, and let's talk again.

Notice how the leader in this example demonstrated an interest in the idea by suggesting a course of action but reserved judgment until the uncertainties are reduced. Responsibility for reducing those uncertainties is placed on the shoulders of the idea generator. If you use a stage-gate system, each gate provides an opportunity to test the validity of ideas and projects in this way. As a leader, you should participate in that system at the most strategic and critical points. In most cases, those will be the initial gates, where the fit with strategic direction is generally determined.

Improve the Idea-to-Commercialization Process

Earlier in this book we described an innovation process that begins with idea generation and then proceeds though various stages that evaluate and develop worthy ideas into commercialized products and services. Like every process, the innovation process should be continually scrutinized for improvement opportunities. Make sure that your process

- Generates a sufficient number of good ideas. If it's not generating enough good ideas, find the root cause and fix it.

- Is free of the bottlenecks that impede development and frustrate innovators.

- Is free of politics.

- Encourages calculated risk taking.

- Is nonarbitrary.

- Creates cheap failures.

- Channels resources to the most worthy projects.

- Involves people who understand the company's capabilities, its strategy, and its customers.

Like cultural change, improving the innovation process is a job for senior management. And it's one of the most important jobs they will ever handle.

Apply Portfolio Thinking

Only the smallest firms deal with one or two development projects. In contrast, big firms may have dozens of funded projects in play at any given time. Some may be low-risk, short-term projects that aim to incrementally improve an existing product. Others may represent a radically new concept that aims to create new markets. Still others may fall between these two extremes. Because incremental and radical projects entail substantial differences in risk levels, time frames, and potential payoffs, management must employ portfolio thinking in dealing with them. Portfolio thinking helps managers to see a collection of ongoing projects in terms of its overall risk/return characteristics. Once they understand those characteristics, they can shape and manage the portfolio to achieve the right balance of risk and potential return.

As a first step toward portfolio thinking, it is often helpful to map ongoing projects onto a two-dimensional matrix like the one in figure 8-1. Here, the horizontal axis indicates the maturity or "newness" of market or technology factors. The vertical axis indicates rising levels of technical challenge, uncertainty, and economic opportunity. Each circle in the matrix represents a project, and the size of each circle indicates the magnitude of resources dedicated to it.

As this matrix indicates, the biggest projects are cautious ones. They have mature technical and market characteristics. Likewise, these

FIGURE 8-1

Innovation Portfolio Matrix

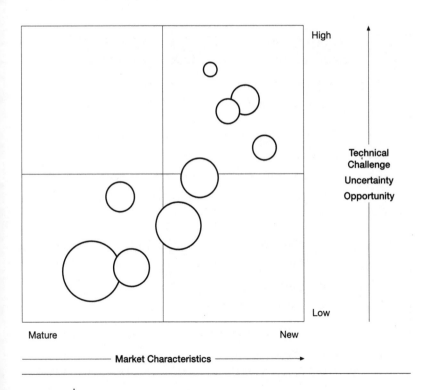

projects are among the least technically challenging and involve the least risk and potential opportunity for the company. Many small projects populate the upper-right quadrant. These involve higher technical risk and address new markets, but they also hold the prospect for greater economic opportunity for the company.

Try constructing a similar matrix for your company. Once you've mapped out your current projects, what does it tell you? If most projects and resources are located in the lower-left quadrant, your company is being very risk averse and may be doing too little to address future opportunities, new technologies, and new markets. On the other hand, if most projects and resources are in the upper-right quadrant, it is being very aggressive. What would constitute a suitable risk/reward balance for your company? Who could articulate that balance?

Tips for Senior Management

- Keep friends and yes-men off the board. You need unvarnished advice as you consider investing in innovative ideas.

- Surround yourself with people who have complementary skills and different approaches to analyzing issues and making decisions. Listen to their suggestions and arguments, even if you disagree. These other voices can help you to avoid walking off a cliff.

- Learn when to cut your losses. To win any game, you must participate. But don't play every game to the end. Recognize when you're pouring resources down a dry hole, and have the fortitude to bail out when you do.

- Always double-check your assumptions. What looks rosy can be a disaster if those assumptions are not realistic.

Put People with the Right Stuff in Charge

Some of the most important decisions that senior executives make involve the selection of R&D managers. These managers are closest to the activities that eventually determine the company's future products and services. But what types of people are most suitable?

Generally, executives should look for people with a balance of strong technical backgrounds and familiarity with the larger concerns of the organization. Specifically, potential R&D managers should (1) have a good feel for the trajectories of technologies important to the company and (2) have practical experience in dealing with customers. Not many people have these two qualities, but those who do are in a much better position to recognize good ideas and understand how they might solve customer problems.

R&D managers are few, even in large organizations. But the general climate for innovation can be improved if executives hire the right middle managers. In her study of innovative middle managers, Rosabeth Moss Kanter found a number of common characteristics. Such managers

- Were comfortable with change

- Viewed unmet needs as opportunities

- Selected projects with great care

- Adopted long time horizons and viewed setbacks as bumps on the road to success

- Were always prepared and professional in making presentations

- Understood organizational politics and where they could get support when needed

- Practiced participative management

These managers could operate with these characteristics, in Kanter's view, because they worked in organizations whose cultures supported collaboration and teamwork and where people were encouraged to "do what needs to be done."[4]

Create an Ambidextrous Organization

Michael Tushman and Charles O'Reilly propose that successful leaders of innovation create "ambidextrous" organizations—that is, organizations that can "get today's work done more effectively and [also] anticipate tomorrow's discontinuities."[5] These are two very different and seemingly contradictory capabilities. Organizations that have them are capable of excelling in the present even as they create the future. They defend their current product or technology positions through incremental innovation while simultaneously developing new ones that will either displace current offerings or address new markets.

Leifer and coworkers reached a similar conclusion in their study of radical innovation in established companies. In their view, the greatest challenge for senior management is balancing their focus on the short-term performance of the existing business as they pursue long-term growth through innovation.[6] These are two very different games, and few companies play both games well. The source of the challenge is not hard to understand. Success in the current business is usually driven by certainty, efficiency, and cost control; the future business, on the other hand, is the product of an innovation process that is uncertain, inefficient, and costly. Not many executives can operate successfully in these two very different worlds. Most are so absorbed with the current business that the future business is treated as a stepchild.

The best way to create an ambidextrous organization is to do the following:

- **Assess where you are in terms of innovation trends.** Are your current products and technologies on the rapid upward slope of the S-curve, or are they in the mature phase of the curve? Do new technologies have the potential to undermine your business?

- **Assess your company's operations.** Are they effective, fast, and efficient? Are major cost improvements possible?

Based on the results of these two assessments, reorder your priorities and resources. You need to be very good at both current operations and innovation.

Summing Up

Although most idea generation and creativity takes place at mid-level and lower ranks, an organization's leaders play a key role. This chapter explained what leaders can do to stimulate creativity and increase the pace of innovation. It is their responsibility to

- Develop a culture that nurtures creativity and innovation

- Establish the strategic direction within which innovation should take place

- Be active participants in the process that runs from idea generation to commercialization

- Be open to new ideas but maintain scientific skepticism

- Improve the idea-to-commercialization process

- Think of ideas and project in terms of a portfolio with distinct risk and return dimensions

- Put the right people in charge

Finally, senior leadership must take responsibility for creating an ambidextrous organization—one that is effective at two very different activities: getting today's work done (operations) and anticipating the future. Few organizations do both well.

The Time Value of Money

Chapter 5 explained how discounted cash flow (DCF) analysis, a financial tool based on time-value-of-money concepts, is often used to evaluate incremental innovation projects. This appendix provides more information on DCF and how it can be directly calculated. It also introduces several related concepts, all of which are valuable in assessing the economic merits of innovations or new products:

- Net present value

- Internal rate of return

- Hurdle rate, discount rate, and the cost of capital

- Sensitivity analysis, a method that increases the practicality of these time-value tools

This material is adapted from *Harvard Business Essentials: Finance for Managers,* another volume in this series.

What Is Time Value?

The time value of money is a mathematically based recognition that money received today is worth more than an equal amount of money received months or years in the future. If you have any doubts about this statement, consider the following example: Your father-in-law takes you aside and says, "The grim reaper is going to catch up with me one of these days. And as much as I'd like to take all of my money with me, I've decided to give you youngsters a bundle of it before I go—say, three hundred thousand dollars."

Naturally, you're pleased to learn of his generous intention. You are also eager to learn *when* the money will be coming your way. "I'm not sure when I'll give you the money," he continues. "It might be this year, next year, or five years down the road. But that shouldn't matter since it will be three hundred thousand in any case."

Your father-in-law got that last point dead wrong. *When* you receive the money does matter. Thanks to the effect of compounding interest, $300,000 put today into a bank CD or savings account with a 5 percent annual interest rate would be worth almost $383,000 five years from now—and slightly more than $483,000 if your investment compounded at a 10 percent annual rate! Let look at how compounding works over time using the $300,000 in our example, with annual compound interest at 10 percent per year over five years (table A-1).

This example demonstrates the importance of time in the receipt of cash amounts. If your father-in-law were to give you the $300,000 today, you'd be $183,153 better off (assuming a 10 percent compounded return) than if he delayed his gift to you by five years. (Note: This analysis assumes that you reinvest the interest you earn at the same rate.)

TABLE A-1

Time Value of an Investment with 10 Percent Compounded Interest

Period	Beginning Value	Interest Earned	Ending Value
1	$300,000	+ $30,000	$330,000
2	$330,000	+ $33,000	$363,000
3	$363,000	+ $36,300	$399,300
4	$399,300	+ $39,930	$439,230
5	$439,230	+ $39,930	$483,153

The example also introduces a number of important terms in the language of finance. The $300,000 is a *present value* (PV), that is, an amount received today. The $483,153 is a *future value* (FV)—the amount to which a present value or series of payments will increase over a specific period at a specific compounding rate. The number of periods (n) in this example is five years. The rate (i) is 10 percent. Understand these terms and you'll probably rise a notch or two in the estimation of your company's CFO.

Generations of business students have been forced to learn how to calculate time values using tables like the one in table A-2. This table indicates the future value of $1, given various compounding rates and compounding periods. Each cell in the table is commonly referred to as a future value interest factor, or FVIF. Tables such as these are easy to use.

TABLE A-2

Future Value of $1 (FVIF)

Periods	8%	9%	10%	11%	12%
1	1.0800	1.0900	1.1000	1.1100	1.1200
2	1.1664	1.1881	1.2100	1.2321	1.2544
3	1.2597	1.2950	1.3310	1.3676	1.4049
4	1.3605	1.4116	1.4641	1.5181	1.5735
5	1.4693	1.5386	1.6105	1.6851	1.7623
6	1.5869	1.6771	1.7716	1.8704	1.9738
7	1.7138	1.8280	1.9487	2.0762	2.2107
8	1.8509	1.9926	2.1436	2.3045	2.4760
9	1.9990	2.1719	2.3579	2.5580	2.7731
10	2.1589	2.3674	2.5937	2.8394	3.1058
11	2.3316	2.5804	2.8531	3.1518	3.4786
12	2.5182	2.8127	3.1384	3.4985	3.8960

The table shows that the FVIF for five periods at 10 percent is 1.6105. Considering the example of the father-in-law's $300,000 gift, we can now find the future value of $300,000 after five years at a 10 percent annual interest rate. To do so, we follow this simple formula:

$$\text{Present Value} \times \text{FVIF} = \text{Future Value}$$

$$\$300{,}000 \times 1.6105 = \$483{,}150$$

This amount is the future value we found earlier using a longhand method (with a slight difference because of rounding).

Every finance text has an appendix of tables that you can use to solve time-value problems. Thanks to today's preprogrammed business calculators and electronic spreadsheets, however, you don't need them. A business calculator such as the ubiquitous Hewlett-Packard 12C has several keys programmed to make these solutions simple. Its keyboard has keys for present value (PV), future value (FV), compounding rate (i), and number of compounding periods (n). If you know any three of these variables, the calculator will solve for the fourth. The instruction book for the calculator explains the sequence to follow in entering the values and obtaining the solution. Likewise, PC spreadsheet programs such as Microsoft's Excel have built-in formulas that make time-value problems easy to solve.

Net Present Value

Future value is an easy idea to grasp, since most of us have been exposed to the principle of compound interest. Put money in an interest-bearing account, leave it alone, and it will grow to a larger amount over time. The longer you leave it alone, or the higher the compounding rate, or both, the larger the future value. The idea of the present value of a future sum is less familiar and less intuitive, but financial people and other savvy managers use it all the time. You can too, and in many types of situations, such as the evaluation of innovative new products.

Present value is the monetary value today of a future payment discounted at some annual compound interest rate. To understand the concept of present value, let's go back to our initial example—the bequest from your father-in-law. In that example, the present value of $483,153 is $300,000. This is calculated through a process of discounting, or reverse compounding, at a rate of 10 percent per year over a period of five years. In the parlance of finance, 10 percent is the *discount rate*. If your father-in-law had said, "I'm planning on giving you $483,153 five years from now, but if you'd rather have the money today I'm willing to give you $300,000," he'd be giving you an equivalent value, assuming you could invest it at 10 percent annually. In short, you would be indifferent regarding the choice of receiving $300,000 now or $483,153 in five years—unless you worried that your father-in-law might not make good on his promise.

As with future value, tables are available for calculating the present value of $1 received in the future. Table A-3 indicates the present value interest factors (PVIFs) for $1 received in the future within a range of discount rates and discounting periods.

TABLE A-3

Present Value of $1 (PVIF)

Period	2%	4%	6%	8%	10%	12%
1	0.980	0.962	0.943	0.926	0.909	0.893
2	0.961	0.925	0.890	0.857	0.826	0.797
3	0.942	0.889	0.840	0.794	0.751	0.712
4	0.924	0.855	0.792	0.735	0.683	0.636
5	0.906	0.822	0.747	0.681	0.621	0.567
6	0.888	0.790	0.705	0.630	0.564	0.507
7	0.871	0.760	0.665	0.583	0.513	0.452
8	0.853	0.731	0.627	0.540	0.467	0.404
9	0.837	0.703	0.592	0.500	0.424	0.361
10	0.820	0.676	0.558	0.463	0.386	0.322

Note that the PVIF for five periods at 10 percent is 0.621. We can use this factor to calculate the present value of your father-in-law's $483,153 gift received five years in the future:

Future Value x PVIF = Present Value

$483,153 x 0.621 = $300,038

We're off by just a little because the PVIF values in the table are rounded.

The PVIF table clearly indicates how the present value of money received in the future shrinks with time. Scan any discount rate column in the PVIF table from top to bottom. The first number is the value of $1 received a year from now. In the 10 percent column, that value is $0.91. The same dollar is worth only $0.39 if you must wait ten years to get your hands on it. Strictly chump change. Notice, too, the role that the discount rate plays in shrinking future values over time. At 6 percent, $1 received ten years from now is worth $0.56. But at a discount rate of 12 percent, that same dollar is down to a mere $0.32!

Your financial calculator and PC spreadsheet can handle this calculation. You simply enter the known values (future value, discount rate, and number of compounding periods) and solve for the unknown value, PV.

Now that you understand present value, let's move on to a typical business situation and see how time-value calculations can help your decision making. But first let's broaden the concept of present value to *net present value* (NPV), which is the present value of one or more future cash flows less any initial investment costs. To illustrate this concept, let's say that Amalgamated Hat Rack Company expects its new product line to start generating $70,000 in annual profit (or, more specifically, net cash flows) beginning one year from now. For simplicity, we'll also say that this level of annual profit will continue for the succeeding five years (totaling $350,000). Bringing the product line onstream will require an up-front investment of $250,000. The questions for the company can thus be phrased as follows: Given this expected profit stream and the $250,000 up-front cost required to produce it, is a new line of coat racks the most productive way to invest that initial $250,000? Or would Amalgamated be better off investing it in something else?

A net present value calculation answers this question by recognizing that the $350,000 in profit that Amalgamated expects to receive over five years is not worth $350,000 in current dollars. Because of the time value of money, it is worth less than that. In other words, that future sum of $350,000 has to be discounted back into an equivalent of today's dollars. How much it is discounted depends on the rate of return Amalgamated could reasonably expect to receive had it chosen to put the initial $250,000 investment into something other than the line of coat racks (but similar in risk) for the same period. As explained earlier, this rate of return is often called the *discount rate*. We define the discount rate as the annual rate, expressed as a percentage, at which a future payment or series of payments is reduced to its present value. In our Amalgamated example, let's assume a discount rate of 10 percent. But before we describe the calculation, let's lay out the situation as follows, with the values in thousands of dollars:

Year	0	1	2	3	4	5
Cash flows	−250	+70	+70	+70	+70	+70

Here we see a negative cash flow of $250,000 in year zero, the starting point of our investment project. This is the cash outflow required to get the project off the ground. The company then experiences a positive cash flow of $70,000 *at the end* of each of the next five years (see the sidebar entitled "Beginning or End of the Period").

Beginning or End of the Period

In solving for net present value and other time-value problems, it is important to know if the cash flows take place at the beginning or end of the period. The present value of a cash flow received in early January is worth more than the same amount received in late December of the same year. Your financial calculator and electronic spreadsheet are set up to accommodate this important difference.

To find the net present value of Amalgamated's stream of cash flows, we need to find the present value of each of the $70,000 cash flows, discounted at 10 percent for the appropriate number of years. If we add together the present values of the five annual inflows and then subtract the $250,000 initially invested, we will have the NPV of the investment. We can determine the NPV for this set of cash flows using the PVIF table in table A-4 and its present value interest factors.

Calculations such as this one can be laborious, but the financial calculators and computer spreadsheets now available make them faster and more accurate. All that you have to do is plug in the right numbers in the right sequence. The NPV function on your calculator or spreadsheet takes into consideration your initial investment, each periodic cash flow, your discount rate, and the number of years over which you will receive the cash flows.

If the resulting NPV is a positive number, and no other investments are under consideration, then the investment should be pursued. In the Amalgamated case depicted in table A-4, the NPV for the line of coat racks is a positive $15,300, which suggests that it would be an attractive investment for Amalgamated. Its compound annual return is at least 10 percent.

TABLE A-4

Net Present Value of Amalgamated's Cash Flow

	Cash Flows (in $1,000)	PVIF	PV (in $1,000)
Year 0	– 250		– 250.00
Year 1	+ 70	0.909	+ 63.63
Year 2	+ 70	0.826	+ 57.82
Year 3	+ 70	0.751	+ 52.57
Year 4	+ 70	0.683	+ 47.81
Year 5	+ 70	0.621	+ 43.47
Total			+ 15.30

Complications

Of course, business situations are almost always more complex than the conveniently simple ones contrived here in the Amalgamated examples. Project investments are rarely made in a single lump sum at the very beginning, and cash flows are almost always irregular— some positive, others negative—over time. What's more, it is often difficult or impossible to accurately estimate what cash flows will look like far in the future, or when they will finally end. Some investments end abruptly with the sale of the product line or factory building—the net sale value of which must be entered as a terminal-value cash flow. Other investments may go on for decades and gradually fade to nothing.

With this complexity in mind, we will try to present a slightly more realistic picture of a business using NPV analysis. Let's deliberately make Amalgamated's new product line investment project slightly more complex. We'll do this in three ways and then show how you could assess the investment project through the same NPV analysis framework.

1. We'll spread the $250,000 investment over three periods instead of one. This is more typical of business practice in developing a new product line.

2. Cash flows will be made more irregular, with a loss in the first full year and growing profitability in later years.

3. We'll arbitrarily plan for Amalgamated to sell the product line at the end of five years for $170,000, and we'll treat the sale price as a terminal value.

Table A–5 shows the results of these assumptions. Using 10 percent as the discount rate, we calculate an NPV of about $69,800 for this series of negative and positive cash flows. If 10 percent is the cost of capital to Amalgamated, we could say that this investment would (1) earn its cost of capital *and* (2) make a positive present-value contribution of $69,800.

TABLE A-5

Net Present Value of Amalgamated's Cash Flow, with Complications (Values in Thousands)

	YEAR					
	0	1	2	3	4	5
Cash Investments	− 150	− 75	− 25	0	0	0
Cash Flow from Operations		− 15	+ 40	+ 80	+ 90	+ 100
Terminal Value						+ 170
Net Cash Flow	− 150	− 90	+ 15	+ 80	+ 90	+ 270
PVIF		0.909	0.826	0.751	0.683	0.621
PV	− 150	− 81.81	+ 12.39	+ 60.08	+ 61.47	+ 167.67
NPV	+ 69.80					

More Complications

Our presentation makes NPV analysis seem as straightforward as the mathematics on which it rests. It *is* straightforward, but the cash flows we use are, unfortunately, merely estimates. Consider Amalgamated's $250,000 investment. Where did that number come from? Chances are it is an agreed-upon estimate produced by people in Amalgamated's research and development and manufacturing units. Those people have experience in designing new products and in setting up the manufacturing equipment needed to crank them out. But past experience is an uncertain guide to the future. The only thing that you can say with certainty is that the cost of the investment will be more or less than $250,000!

Estimates of the net cash flows from operations are bound to be even less certain. Consider how cash flow from operations is determined. The product line manager no doubt asks the marketing department three questions:

1. How many of these new products (in units) can your people sell in each of the next five years?

2. What would be our net revenues from each sale?

3. What level of marketing budget would you need to achieve those sales at those prices?

The manager would likewise get a unit production and labor and materials cost estimate from the manufacturing unit. In effect, the new-product manager would have to develop a detailed "mini" income statement. This statement would detail the revenues and costs (i.e., materials, labor, marketing, and all other costs) associated with the new product line over the five-year span of the analysis. The sum of the revenues and costs would be the cash flow from operations.

Taken together, these annual estimated cash flows from operations would be used in determining the NPV of the project. Obviously, there are lots of assumptions here, and plenty of room for error—especially as people attempt to forecast sales further and further into the future. There is even a chance that sales of the new product line will cannibalize the sales of existing product lines. As a consequence, opponents of the particular investment can usually find lots of opportunities to take potshots at the numbers, and experienced decision makers usually insist on fairly conservative sales forecasts and cost estimates.

Nevertheless, careful NPV analysis based on sound assumptions is an excellent decision-making tool—and it's certainly better than the alternatives. Its value can be improved if the NPV of an investment is presented in worst-case, most-likely-case, and best-case scenarios. This approach captures a broader range of opinions in the organization about future unit sales, various costs of production, and other assumptions.

Internal Rate of Return

The *internal rate of return* (IRR) is another tool that managers can use to decide whether to commit to a particular investment opportunity, or to rank the desirability of various opportunities. IRR is defined as the discount rate at which the NPV of an investment equals zero. Let's consider what that means in terms of our more complicated version of Amalgamated's cash flow projection for its new product line:

Year	0	1	2	3	4	5
Net cash flow	−150	-90	+15	+80	+90	+270

As calculated earlier, the NPV of this stream of cash flows discounted at 10 percent was a positive $69,800. That told us that these numbers, if realized, would cover Amalgamated's cost of capital (10 percent) *and* contribute an additional present value of $69,800. IRR tells us something more. It captures the discount rate *and* the additional present-value contribution in a single number. To calculate it, we need to determine the discount rate that would reduce NPV to exactly zero. IRR is that discount rate.

We know right off the bat that the IRR for our example must be greater than 10 percent because the cash flow discounted at 10 percent produced a positive NPV. But how much more? Well, if we had a few blackboards and several hours, we could calculate the IRR through an iterative process that used higher and higher discount rates. Eventually, we'd get to the one that produced an NPV of zero. But financial calculators and electronic spreadsheets again come to the rescue, making IRR calculations very easy. All we need to do is enter the values for each of the cash flows and solve for the discount rate (i). The IRR calculation is based on the same algebraic formula as the NPV calculation. With the NPV calculation, you know the discount rate, or the desired rate of return, and are solving the equation for the NPV of the future cash flows. In contrast, with IRR, the NPV is set at zero and the discount rate is unknown. The equation solves for the discount rate. For the Amalgamated project just described, the IRR is about 17.7 percent.

Typically, when the IRR is greater than the opportunity cost (the expected return on a comparable investment) of the capital required, the investment under consideration should be undertaken. You can use your company's hurdle rate as the IRR target. The *hurdle rate* is a minimal rate of return that all investments for a particular enterprise must achieve; this rate is usually prescribed by the CFO.

The IRR of the investment under consideration must exceed the hurdle rate in order for the company to go forward with it.

What's a reasonable hurdle rate for a business? It varies from company to company. Typically, the hurdle rate is set well above what could be obtained from a risk-free investment, such as a U.S. Treasury bond. You can, in fact, think of the hurdle rate as follows:

Hurdle Rate =
Risk-Free Rate + Premium That Reflects the Enterprise's Risk

Like any investor, a business entity expects to be rewarded for the uncertainty to which it is subjected. New product lines and other such activities are, by nature, filled with uncertainty. For this reason, business entities demand that prospective projects show particularly good promise.

Some companies use different hurdle rates for different types of investments, with low-risk investments having to clear a lower hurdle than that imposed on the higher-risk type. For example, a company might require that replacement of an existing assembly line or a specialized piece of equipment use a hurdle rate of 8 percent, whereas the expansion of an existing product line would use a 12 percent hurdle rate. The development of a new product line, which is riskier still, might require a 15 percent hurdle rate.

Hurdle Rate and the Cost of Capital

We have defined the hurdle rate as the minimal rate of return that all investments for a particular enterprise must achieve. The firm's *cost of capital* is more specific. It is the weighted average cost of the organization's different sources of capital: both debt and equity.

Everyone understands that the debt capital employed by corporations has a cost—namely, the interest paid on bonds and other IOUs. Few nonfinancial people think of the capital contributed by owners as having a real cost, but it does. This cost is an opportunity cost—what the shareholders could earn on their capital if they invested in the next-best opportunity available to them at the same level of risk.

The methodology for calculating the cost of capital for an individual business or for business units is beyond the scope of this book. Put simply, however, the cost of capital is the weighted average cost of the organization's different sources of capital.

From a practical standpoint, you might equate your company's cost of capital with the hurdle rate mentioned in our discussion of NPV. The CFO can provide this number but will likely adjust the hurdle rate upward for projects of increasing risk.

Sensitivity Analysis

Every business forecast includes one or more assumptions. In proposing the company's new coat-rack line, Amalgamated managers no doubt assumed that its dealers would pay x dollars per unit, that materials costs would be y dollars per unit, and that the investment needed to get the operation off the ground would be z dollars. These are just a few of many assumptions.

What would happen if one or more of these assumptions failed to hold? Sensitivity analysis helps you to ask just that question and to see the ramifications of incremental changes in the assumptions that underlie a particular projection. The starting point for sensitivity analysis is in the underlying assumptions. If you are looking at breakeven analysis, take another look at your assumptions about each of the key critical components:

- **Fixed costs and variable costs.** Are you certain that your estimates for these costs are on target? Get the views of others on this, and try to establish a range of likely cost scenarios. Point estimates are almost always wrong.

- **Contribution.** The unit contribution is based on the selling price less the unit variable cost. Thus, if you're looking at a new product or service, chances are that the selling price is still to be tested. Question the validity of that assumption. If your product or service will be very similar to others already on the market, then the price that people are already paying may be a reliable guide. But if your product or service is new to the world, then there may have been some guesswork involved in the determination of the selling price—even if your company conducted customer research. So again, it's a good idea to establish a range of likely selling prices for the new product or service.

You can perform the same type of sensitivity analysis on NPV calculations. In the Amalgamated case, for instance, you'd want to look more closely at the positive cash flows forecasted in years 1 through 5. Most people cannot accurately forecast next year's cash flows, let alone those that occur many years in the future. Current estimates may not be reliable. Careful study may reveal a range of possible cash flows, with that range widening with each passing year.

Once you've determined a range of possible cash flows for each year of the analysis, calculate the NPV for the best case, the worst case, and the most likely case. This will help your senior executives make a better decision. It will also help everyone understand which assumptions make or break the investment itself. These might be the selling price, the timing of the new product launch, or the cost of raw materials. Management can then focus its time and energy on making more accurate forecasts regarding those items, and once the project is in play, management will know that it must give those important points the greatest attention.

Useful Implementation Tools

This appendix contains three forms (exhibits B-1, B-2, and B-3) that you may find useful when planning and encouraging innovation. All are adapted from Harvard ManageMentor, an online help source for subscribers. For interactive versions of these worksheets, please visit http://www.elearning.hbsp.org/businesstools. Downloadable forms, checklists, and other useful tools found in the *Harvard Business Essentials* series can be found on that site.

1. **Workplace Assessment Checklist (exhibit B-1).** How friendly is your workplace to creativity and innovation? This checklist will help you make an assessment. Suggestion: Photocopy the checklist, and then have several people fill in the ratings independently. Then compare answers. This will help you see the workplace—and yourself—as others do.

2. **Assessing the Psychological Environment (exhibit B-2).** Use this checklist to assess how your current reward structure, group norms and attitudes, and management style support creativity.

3. **Planning for Innovation (exhibit B-3).** Innovation is an outcome of the creative process and involves identifying and implementing new ideas. Use this tool to help plan how an idea will be rolled out and to identify the critical factors needed for it to be accepted.

EXHIBIT B-1

Workplace Assessment Checklist

Dimension	Rating *Adequate*	 *A Strength*	 *Needs Improvement*
Your Leadership Style I can describe my own preferred style of thinking and working.			
I have talked with members of my group about their preferred modes of problem solving.			
I encourage intellectual conflict within my group.			
When group members disagree, I help them determine the source of their differences.			
When communicating with others, I take into consideration their preferred thinking style.			
Diversity of Styles I am aware of the creative value of diverse thinking styles and try to incorporate this diversity in teams.			
I actively seek out or hire people with diverse backgrounds and thinking styles.			
Our group recognizes the conflict that creative abrasion can cause but also recognizes its value.			
We have taken formal diagnostic tests to identify thinking or learning styles and discussed the results of these assessments.			
Your Work Group The majority never ignores the minority opinions in my work group.			
I have added someone to my work group specifically because he or she brings a fresh perspective.			
Our work environment supports those who think differently from the majority.			
The thinking styles, skills, and experiences of my work group's members are diverse and balanced.			
I actively look for group members whose thinking styles differ from my own.			
I help my group establish and agree upon a clear project goal at the start of each project.			
My group has formally agreed-upon behavior guidelines for how they should work together and treat each other.			

EXHIBIT B-1

Workplace Assessment Checklist

Dimension	Adequate	A Strength	Needs Improvement
The Psychological Environment			
I support people taking intelligent risks and do not penalize them when they fail.			
There are opportunities for people to take on assignments that involve risk and stretch their potential.			
We openly discuss risk taking, assess the risk potential of projects, and make contingency plans or identify risk management strategies.			
Rewards and/or recognition are given for creative ideas.			
As long as they show learning from the experience, group members are not penalized for experimentation and risk taking.			
The Physical Workspace			
Our workspace includes stimulating objects such as journals, art, and other items that are not directly related to our business.			
I have made changes to our physical workspace to improve communication and creative interaction.			
I provide group members with a wide variety of traditional and nontraditional communication tools (e-mail, whiteboards, crayons and paper, etc.).			
Group members are encouraged to make their workspaces reflect their individuality.			
Our workspace includes *both* areas for boisterous interaction *and* areas for quiet reflection.			

EXHIBIT B-1

Workplace Assessment Checklist

		Rating	
Dimension	*Adequate*	*A Strength*	*Needs Improvement*
Bringing in Outsiders or Alternative Perspectives			
Our group makes visits to people outside the division or organization in order to find different perspectives and ideas.			
Our group has observed customers actually using our product or service *in their own environment.*			
Our group has observed our customers' customers using our product or service *in their own environment.*			
I have arranged for speakers from other industries to come talk to or work with my group.			
Our group has observed people using competitors' products or services.			
Our group has benchmarked the functions and characteristics of our products, services, or internal processes against an industry other than our own.			
Promoting Group Convergence			
I encourage group members to bring up and discuss non-work-related subjects when they interfere with work.			
When a project has been completed, I hold a debrief meeting to determine specifically what to do differently (or the same) the next time.			
When I hold a debrief meeting, I always make sure that all members can be present.			
When my group is stuck on a problem, I make sure they get "down time" or time off to step back, relax, and allow their subconscious minds to work.			
At the end of a project, I provide a way for my group to celebrate and rejuvenate.			
Project schedules allow enough time for group brainstorming and discussion of ideas.			

Source: HMM Managing for Creativity and Innovation.

EXHIBIT B-2

Assessing the Psychological Environment

Question	Rating Adequate	A Strength	Needs Improvement
1. Are group guidelines already in place? Are they articulated and disseminated?			
2. Do you, as the manager, encourage risk taking?			
3. Are people allowed to take intelligent risks, and fail, without being penalized?			
4. When someone fails, do you help him and the group find the learning in the failure?			
5. Do you distinguish between intelligent failures (something risky, but promising) and mistakes (something clearly avoidable)?			
6. Do your current rewards motivate group members to be creative?			
7. Do you currently have rewards for creative ideas or suggestions?			
8. Do you have both extrinsic (for example, money) and intrinsic (for example, providing a sense of accomplishment) rewards in your current reward system?			
9. Do you recognize group members who successfully work outside their preferred thinking style or area of expertise?			
10. Do you support intellectual conflict within your group?			
11. Do you encourage people to point out unacknowledged and taboo subjects that are holding the group back?			
12. Do you reward collaboration?			
13. Do individuals have freedom to choose their projects or to determine how they reach their agreed-upon goals?			
14. Are you, as a manager, alert to individuals who may be burning out?			
15. Do you celebrate small successes?			
16. Do you encourage the group to stop and review how much progress it has made?			

Ideas for Improvement

Based on your answers, what refinements would you make to your group's norms? To your reward structure? To your own management style?

Source: HMM Managing for Creativity and Innovation.

Planning for Innovation

Idea: **Date:**

Generated by:

Innovation *(what form the idea will take):*

Sources of Support

What sources of assistance or support are needed to carry out this innovation?

Who	Why Needed

What (money, resources, etc.)

Ways to gain and strengthen support

Sources of Resistance

What are the sources of resistance—people to policies, procedures, and so forth—that could impede the process of innovation?

Who	Why

What (for example, organizational policy)

Ways to overcome or minimize resistance

EXHIBIT B - 3

Planning for Innovation

Immediate Goals and Actions Planned

Goal/Action   *Completion Date*

Measures of Success

1.	*6.*
2.	*7.*
3.	*8.*
4.	*9.*
5.	*10*

Target Long-Term Actions

Action   *Completion Date*

Source: HMM Managing for Creativity and Innovation.

Notes

Chapter 1

1. The story of the silicon germanium chip and its innovator is ably told in various sections of Richard Leifer, Christopher McDermott, Gina Colarelli O'Connor, Lois Peters, Mark Rice, and Robert Veryzer, *Radical Innovation* (Boston: Harvard Business School Press, 2000).

2. Ibid., 5.

3. Lee A. Sage, *Winning the Innovation Race* (New York: John Wiley & Sons, 2000), 7.

4. Michael L. Tushman and Charles A. O'Reilly III, *Winning Through Innovation* (Boston: Harvard Business School Press, 1997), 160–161.

5. Leifer et al., *Radical Innovation*.

6. Procter & Gamble's development of the disposable diaper is told in Oscar Schisgall, *Eyes on Tomorrow* (Chicago: J.G. Ferguson, 1981), 216–220.

Chapter 2

1. See Richard Foster, *Innovation: The Attacker's Advantage* (New York: Summit Books, 1986).

2. Clayton Christensen, interview with Harvard Business School Publishing, <http://www.hbsp.harvard.edu/products/pressbooks/innovator/qa. html> (accessed 8 October 1998).

3. Michael L. Tushman and Charles A. O'Reilly III, *Winning Through Innovation* (Boston: Harvard Business School Press, 1997), 17.

Chapter 3

1. Peter F. Drucker, "The Discipline of Innovation," *Harvard Business Review*, May–June 1985, 67–72.

2. "Solving the Innovator's Dilemma," *Product Development Best Practices Report,* May 2000. Available at <http://www.managementroundtable.com/ PDBPR/stategyn.html>.

3. Dorothy Leonard and Jeffrey F. Rayport, "Spark Innovation Through Empathetic Design," *Harvard Business Review,* November–December 1997, 102–113.

4. Richard Leifer, Christopher McDermott, Gina Colarelli O'Connor, Lois Peters, Mark Rice, and Robert Veryzer, *Radical Innovation* (Boston: Harvard Business School Press, 2000), 142–155.

5. Lee A. Sage, *Winning the Innovation Race* (New York: John Wiley & Sons, 2000), 15–16.

6. Darrell Rigby and Chris Zook, "Open Market Innovation," *Harvard Business Review,* October 2002, 80–89.

7. Albert Shapiro, "Creativity and the Management of Creative Professionals," *Research-Technology Management,* March–April 1985.

8. Edward Roberts and Alan Fusfeld, "Critical Functions: Needed Roles in the Innovation Process," in *The Human Side of Managing Technological Innovation,* ed. Ralph Katz (New York: Oxford University Press, 1997), 279.

9. For a more complete description of catchball, see George Labovitz and Victor Rosansky, *The Power of Alignment* (New York: John Wiley & Sons, 1997), 90–92.

Chapter 4

1. "Norman R. Augustine, 1997," The Spirit of American Innovation: The National Medal of Technology, 31 July 2002, <http://www.thetech.org/exhibits/online/nmot/>.

2. For more on DuPont's experience with Biomax, see Richard Leifer, Christopher McDermott, Gina Colarelli O'Connor, Lois Peters, Mark Rice, and Robert Veryzer, *Radical Innovation* (Boston: Harvard Business School Press, 2000), 12–16.

3. W. Chan Kim and Renée Mauborgne, "Knowing a Winning Business Idea When You See One," *Harvard Business Review,* September–October 2000, 129–136, 138.

4. Leifer et al., *Radical Innovation,* 35.

Chapter 5

1. For a more complete development of this issue, see Don Reinertsen, "There Is No Fun in the Funnel," *Product Development Best Practices Report,* October 1999. Available at <http://www.managementroundtable.com/PDBPR/Funnell.html>.

2. Robert G. Cooper, "Stage-Gate Systems: A New Tool for Managing New Products," *Business Horizons,* May–June 1990, 45–54.

3. Robert G. Cooper, "Selecting Winning New Product Projects," *Journal of Product Innovation Management,* February 1985, 35.

4. Clayton Christensen, interview with Harvard Business School Publishing, <http://www.hbsp.harvard.edu/products/pressbooks/innovator/qa.html> (accessed 8 October 1998).

5. Marc H. Meyer and Alvin P. Lehnerd, *The Power of Product Platforms* (New York: The Free Press, 1997), xii.

6. Ibid., 5–15.

Chapter 6

1. Albert Shapiro, "Managing Creative Professionals," *Research-Technology Management,* March–April 1985.

2. Teresa M. Amabile, "How to Kill Creativity," *Harvard Business Review,* September–October 1998, 77–87.

3. Teresa M. Amabile, Constance N. Hadley, and Steven J. Kramer, "Creativity Under the Gun," *Harvard Business Review,* August 2002, 57.

Chapter 7

1. "Inspiring Innovation," *Harvard Business Review,* August 2002, 49.

2. Ibid., 40.

3. Lee Sage, *Winning the Innovation Race* (New York: John Wiley & Sons, 2000), 150–151.

4. For an excellent description of the Xerox and L.L. Bean case, see Gregory H. Watson, *Strategic Benchmarking* (New York: John Wiley & Sons, 1993), 149–167.

5. Richard Leifer, Christopher McDermott, Gina Colarelli O'Connor, Lois Peters, Mark Rice, and Robert Veryzer, *Radical Innovation* (Boston: Harvard Business School Press, 2000), 162–163.

6. "McKnight Principles," 3M.com, <http://www.3m.com/profile/looking/mcknightl.jhtml> (accessed 19 April 2002).

7. See Turid Horgen, Donald A. Schon, William L. Porter, and Michael L. Joroff, *Excellence by Design* (New York: John Wiley & Sons, 1998).

8. Thomas J. Allen, "Communication Networks in R&D Labs," *R&D Management* 1 (1971): 14–21.

Chapter 8

1. Michael L. Tushman and Charles A. O'Reilly III, *Winning Through Innovation* (Boston: Harvard Business School Press, 1997), 33–34.

2. Mike Beer, "Leading Change," class note 9-488-037, Harvard Business School Publishing, Boston, revised 15 May 1991, 2.

3. Kim Clark and Steven Wheelwright, *Revolutionizing Product Development* (New York: Free Press, 1992), 31–34.

4. Rosabeth Moss Kanter, "The Middle Manager as Innovator," *Harvard Business Review*, July–August 1982, 95–105.

5. Tushman and O'Reilly, *Winning Through Innovation,* 219.

6. Richard Leifer, Christopher McDermott, Gina Colarelli O'Connor, Lois Peters, Mark Rice, and Robert Veryzer, *Radical Innovation* (Boston: Harvard Business School Press, 2000).

Glossary

BREAKEVEN ANALYSIS   A form of analysis that helps determine how much (or how much more) a company needs to sell in order to pay for the fixed investment—in other words, at what point the company will break even on its cash flow.

BREAKTHROUGH INNOVATION   See *Radical innovation.*

CATCHBALL   A cross-functional method for accomplishing two things: idea enrichment or improvement, and buy-in among participants.

COMMUNITY OF INTEREST   An informal group whose members share an interest in some technology or application.

CONTRIBUTION MARGIN   The amount of money that every sold unit contributes to paying for fixed costs. It is defined as net unit revenue minus variable (or direct) costs per unit.

CONVERGENT THINKING   Thinking that evaluates new ideas to determine which are genuinely novel and worth pursuing.

COST OF CAPITAL   The weighted average cost of the organization's different sources of capital, both debt and equity.

CREATIVITY   A process of developing and expressing novel ideas that are likely to be useful.

DISCONTINUOUS INNOVATION   See *Radical innovation.*

DISCOUNT RATE   In discounted cash flow analysis, the annual rate, expressed as a percentage, at which a future payment or series of payments is reduced to its present value.

DISCOUNTED CASH FLOW ANALYSIS   A method for determining the monetary value of a commercial idea over a particular span of time based on time-value-of-money concepts.

DISRUPTIVE TECHNOLOGY   A technical innovation that has the potential to upset the status quo and, as it develops and is perfected, displaces the established technology and precipitates the decline of leading companies.

DIVERGENT THINKING   Thinking that breaks away from familiar or established ways of seeing and doing.

EMPATHETIC DESIGN   An idea-generating technique whereby innovators observe how people use existing products and services in their own environments.

EXTRINSIC REWARD   A reward that appeals to a person's desire for attainment distinct from the work itself, such as a cash bonus, a promotion, or stock options.

FIXED COSTS   Costs that stay mostly the same, no matter how many units of a product or service are sold, such as the cost of product development, insurance, management salaries, and rent or lease payments.

FUTURE VALUE   In discounted cash flow analysis, the amount to which a present value or series of payments will increase over a specific period at a specific compounding rate.

GROUPTHINK   The tendency of individual thought to converge for social reasons around a particular point of view.

HURDLE RATE   The minimal rate of return that all investments for a particular enterprise must achieve.

IDEA FUNNEL   A concept used in product development to illustrate the way in which many innovative ideas are gradually reduced to a very few that proceed to commercialization.

INCREMENTAL INNOVATION   Innovation that either improves upon something that already exists or reconfigures an existing form or technology to serve some other purpose. In this sense it is innovation at the margins.

INNOVATION   The embodiment, combination, or synthesis of knowledge in original, relevant, valued new products, processes, or services.

INTERNAL RATE OF RETURN (IRR)   The discount rate at which the net present value of an investment equals zero.

INTRINSIC REWARD   A reward that appeals to a person's desire for self-actualization, curiosity, enjoyment, or interest in the work itself.

LEAD USER   Company or individual whose needs are far ahead of market trends.

NET PRESENT VALUE (NPV)   The present value of one or more future cash flows less any initial investment.

OPEN MARKET INNOVATION   The practice of reaching outside one's company for new product and service ideas.

OPPORTUNITY RECOGNITION   A mental process that answers the question: Does this idea represent real value to current or potential customers?

PRESENT VALUE   In discounted cash flow analysis, the amount received today; the monetary value today of a future payment discounted at some annual compound interest rate.

PRODUCT PLATFORM   A set of subsystems and interfaces that form a common structure from which a stream of derivative products can be efficiently developed and produced.

RADICAL INNOVATION   An innovation that represents something new to the world and a departure from existing technologies or methods. Also referred to as *breakthrough innovation* and *discontinuous innovation*.

S-CURVE   A plot on a two-dimensional plane that describes the performance or cost characteristics of a technology change with time and continued investments.

SKUNKWORKS   A team of people brought together in one place to generate an innovative solution or to solve a particular problem. In some cases, skunkworks are sited in remote settings to keep team members focused on their mission, to minimize interference from the rest of the organization, or to maintain secrecy.

STAGE-GATE SYSTEM   An alternating series of development stages and assessment gates that aims for early elimination of losing ideas and faster time-to-market for potential winners.

THINKING STYLE   The unconscious way in which a person looks at and interacts with the world.

VARIABLE COSTS   Those costs that change with the number of units produced and sold; examples include utilities, labor, and the costs of raw materials.

For Further Reading

Barrett, Derm. *The Paradox Process.* New York: AMACOM, 1997. Paradoxical thinking comprises three essential skills: the ability to break free from conventional thought patterns, the ability to identify opposites and juxtapose them, and the ability to integrate opposites to form new solutions. This book describes these skills and also provides techniques for improving each of them.

Csikszentmihalyi, Mihaly. *Creativity: Flow and the Psychology of Discovery and Invention.* New York: HarperCollins, 1996. Csikszentmihalyi focuses on the creativity of exceptional people—the paradoxical traits they possess and the unique aspects of their development over the life cycle—but he also suggests ways for enhancing creativity in everyday life.

Davis, Howard, and Richard Scase. *Managing Creativity: The Dynamics of Work and Organization.* Buckingham, England: Open University Press, 2001. The creative industries are a growing economic as well as cultural force. This book investigates their organizational dynamics and shows how companies structure their work processes to incorporate creative employees' needs for autonomy while at the same time controlling and coordinating their output.

Harvard Business School Publishing. *Continuous Innovation: No Genius Required.* Harvard Business Review OnPoint Collection. Boston: Harvard Business School Publishing, 2001. This collection of three *Harvard Business Review* articles shows you how to approach innovation by systematically (1) generating new possibilities through applying old, proven ideas to new situations; (2) gathering additional ideas by identifying and learning from individuals and companies well ahead of market trends; and (3) testing the merits of those ideas through rapid, inexpensive experimentation.

Harvard Business School Publishing. *Harvard Business Review on Breakthrough Thinking.* Harvard Business Review Paperback Series. Boston: Harvard Business School Press, 1999. This collection of *Harvard Business Review* articles highlights leading ideas for incorporating the power of creativity into your strategic outlook.

Katz, Ralph, ed. *The Human Side of Managing Technological Innovation*. 2d ed. New York: Oxford University Press, 2002. This collection of articles hits all the bases that a manager of innovation must understand, such as how to motivate R&D professionals and how to manage innovative groups, project teams, and organizational projects. A handy reference for the important people part of innovation.

Kim, W. Chan, and Renée Mauborgne. "Knowing a Winning Idea When You See One." *Harvard Business Review*, September–October 2000. Identifying which business ideas have real commercial potential is fraught with uncertainty. This article introduces three tools that managers can use to help strip away some of that uncertainty. The first is the buyer utility map (described in chapter 4 of this book). The second, the price corridor of the mass, identifies what price will unlock the greatest number of customers. The third, the business model guide, offers a framework for figuring out whether and how a company can profitably deliver the new idea at the targeted price.

Leifer, Richard, Christopher M. McDermott, Gina Colarelli O'Connor, Lois Peters, Mark Rice, and Robert Veryzer. *Radical Innovation: How Mature Companies Can Outsmart Upstarts*. Boston: Harvard Business School Press, 2000. This book reveals the patterns through which game-changing innovation occurs in large, established companies, and identifies the new managerial competencies firms need to make radical innovation happen. The authors, experts in a variety of areas such as entrepreneurship, R&D management, product design, marketing, organizational behavior, and operations and project management, distill a comprehensive, interdisciplinary approach to mastering each of these challenges, from the conceptualization of viable ideas to the commercialization of radical innovations.

Leonard, Dorothy, and Walter Swap. *When Sparks Fly: Igniting Creativity in Groups*. Boston: Harvard Business School Press, 1999. Where do the best creative ideas come from? Most managers assume that it's the readily identifiable "creative types" who offer the quickest route to out-of-the-box, breakthrough thinking, and that if you don't have an eccentric genius on your team, your group is doomed to mediocrity. Yet, say Leonard and Swap, most innovations today spring from well-led group interactions. In *When Sparks Fly*, the authors reveal that any group—if designed and managed effectively—can produce innovative services, products, and processes. Unlike most books on creativity, *When Sparks Fly* focuses on the process as it applies to groups of people who may not fit the

stereotype of right-brained "creatives." Leonard and Swap offer managers strategies for generating the group dynamics that lie at the heart of
innovative thinking, including specific techniques for rechanneling the
tensions of conflicting points of view into new ideas and alternative options. *When Sparks Fly* explores how all aspects of the work environment, from leadership style to the use of space, sound, even smell, can
enhance innovation.

Michalko, Michael. *Cracking Creativity: The Secrets of Creative Genius.* Berkeley, CA: Ten Speed Press, 1998. Michalko divides the topic into two sections—seeing what no one else sees and thinking what no one else is
thinking—and provides concrete examples, strategies, and exercises for
each. For example, strategies for novel thinking include connecting the
unconnected, looking at the other side, and finding what you're not
looking for.

Miller, William C. *Flash of Brilliance.* Reading, MA: Perseus Books, 1999.
Miller emphasizes the ways in which an individual's values and spiritu-
ality enrich and inform his or her creativity. The book also includes concrete suggestions for overcoming obstacles to creativity and provides an
extended treatment of four basic approaches to brainstorming.

Robinson, Alan G., and Sam Stern. *Corporate Creativity.* San Francisco:
Berrett-Koehler, 1997. An in-depth analysis of six elements that make for
creativity in the work environment: alignment, self-initiated activity, unofficial activity, serendipity, diverse stimuli, and in-company communication.

von Hippel, Eric. *The Sources of Innovation.* New York: Oxford University
Press, 1997. This book presents studies showing that end users, material
suppliers, and others—and not always manufacturers—are the typical
sources of innovation in some fields. These finding suggest that R&D
people should search out lead users as sources of innovative ideas. von
Hippel, Stefan Thomke, and Mary Sonnack explore a practical process
for working with lead users in "Creating Breakthroughs at 3M," *Harvard
Business Review*, September–October 1999, 47–57.

Zelinski, Ernie J. *The Joy of Thinking Big.* Berkeley, CA: Ten Speed Press,
1998. This book lacks a cohesive conceptual framework, but its strength
lies in the dozens of hands-on tips and strategies for individuals that get
at the heart of the creative paradox. Sample topics include how to develop a great memory for forgetting, how to fail successfully, and how to
be a creative loafer.

Index

About the Subject Adviser

DR. RALPH KATZ is a professor of management at Northeastern University's College of Business and is in the Management of Technology Group of M.I.T.'s Sloan School of Management. He has carried out extensive management research on technology-based innovation with emphasis in the management of technical professionals and project teams.

The National Academy of Management awarded Dr. Katz the "New Concept Award" for his significant contribution to the field of organizational behavior. He is also a recipient of several of R&D Management's "Best Paper" awards.

Dr. Katz's most recent book publication is *The Human Side of Managing Technological Innovation*. He is the R&D/Innovation and Entrepreneurship Departmental Editor for *Management Science*. He received his Ph.D. and M.B.A. from the University of Pennsylvania's Wharton Graduate School and a B.S. in mathematics from Carnegie Mellon University.

About the Writer

RICHARD LUECKE is the writer of several books in the Harvard Business Essentials series. Based in Salem, Massachusetts, Mr. Luecke has authored or developed over thirty books and dozens of articles on a wide range of business subjects. He has an M.B.A. from the University of St. Thomas.